How To Own Your Own Mind

BECOMING EPICALLY DECISIVE

Become A Master Of Yourself And Achieve Your Greatest Potential

Hazel Ford

Table of Contents

Chapter 1: How Not To Waste Your 25,000 Mornings As An Adult... 6
Chapter 2: How To Focus on Creating Positive Actions 8
Chapter 3: 6 Ways to Start All Over Again 11
Chapter 4: *How to Stop Chasing New Goals All the Time* 15
Chapter 5: Six Steps To Create A Vision For Your Life........................... 18
Chapter 6: *Why You Should Master One Thing AT a time*....................... 22
Chapter 7: Dealing with Career Pressure.. 25
Chapter 8: 6 Steps To Get Out of Your Comfort Zone 28
Chapter 9: 10 Habits of Emma Stone... 34
Chapter 10: 5 Tips to Doing Unique and Meaningful Work 38
Chapter 11: Believe in Yourself 42
Chapter 12: Five Steps to Clarify Your Goals 44
Chapter 13: Consistency can bring you happiness.................................... 48
Chapter 14: Why You're Demotivated By A Values Conflict................. 53
Chapter 15: It's Not Your Job to Tell Yourself "No" 56
Chapter 16: Dealing with Difficult Bosses.. 59
Chapter 17: NOTHING IS IMPOSSIBLE 62
Chapter 18: 7 Ways To Develop Effective Communication With Your Clients.. 65
Chapter 19: Stop Lying To Yourself... 69
Chapter 20: How Successful People Figure What To Focus On 72
Chapter 21: HOW TO AVOID BURNOUT 75
Chapter 22: 10 Habits of Meryl Streep 78
Chapter 23: Become A High Performer... 82
Chapter 24: *The Downside of Work-Life Balance* 86
Chapter 25: 10 Habits to Change Your Life 89
Chapter 26: 8 Ways To Gain Self-Confidence 96
Chapter 27: *7 Ways To Discover Your Strengths*...................................... 100

Chapter 28: 7 Ways To Know When It's Time To Say Goodbye To The Past 105
Chapter 29: Dealing With Addictions 109
Chapter 30: Happy People Dream Big 112
Chapter 31: *Be Motivated by Challenge* 114
Chapter 32: 10 Habits of Adele 117
Chapter 33: Why Are You Working So Hard 121
Chapter 34: Happy People Live Slow 125
Chapter 35: Six Ways To Track Your Habits 127

Chapter 1:
How Not To Waste Your 25,000 Mornings As An Adult.

Adulthood is the time of our lives when we need to get serious about everything. We have to take care of every single thing from time to our mornings. Early morning is the time of the day when freshness consumes us—known as the best time to work. Why waste such precious time? Having a good morning automatically means having a good day too. When a mind is fresh, it works. And wasting 25,000 mornings of your adulthood would be truly foolish. Those 3571 weeks would go to waste as there was no essential work done.

To make sure that you don't waste your morning is to be sure that you have mornings. Waking up late just automatically means that half of your day has gone to waste. So, wake up early. Those early hours have some courage to work in them. And who wants to waste such an opportunity to prove themselves. Not only will it be beneficial for your professional life, but it will also be beneficial for your health. Get a decent night's sleep, and you will see the changes that come along with them.

After you open your eyes in the morning, immediately sit up. Going back to sleep is always a more intriguing option. But we need to know that our priority is to wake up. And when you are sleeping, make sure that nothing disturbs it. Phone on silent—the tv's off and lights out. Make sure you are as comfortable as possible so you won't wake up the following day grumpy. Disturbance in sleep may cause the disappearance of it. There is a chance that you can't sleep again. That is not what we want. So, we take things beforehand.

An easy way to wake up in the morning is to have some encouragement ready for you. Either it's gym or work. It will make you wake up in the morning early to jump-start whatever you have planned. Then the mornings will be a lot more efficient for you and much more enjoyable. The first thing that we tend to do right after waking up is to check our phones. We waste 20 minutes or more just lying there doing nothing much of a task. Let's get one thing clear. It's not worth it. Wake up in the morning, get a cup of coffee, and start your day without any technology, naturally.

Once you fall into a habit, you will fall into a routine. Your life will change for the good, and you will look towards the brighter side of life. Mornings are a precious time, and 25,000 of our adulthood is the most important morning of our life. So, make sure that you make every morning out of those 25,000 mornings count. It won't be easy, but it will be worth it!

Chapter 2:
How To Focus on Creating Positive Actions

Only a positive person can lead a healthy life. Imagine waking up every day feeling like you are ready to face the day's challenges and you are filled with hope about life. That is something an optimist doesn't have to imagine because they already feel it every day. Also, scientifically, it is proven that optimistic people have a lower chance of dying because of a stress-caused disease. Although positive thinking will not magically vanish all your problems, it will make them seem more manageable and somewhat not a big deal.

Positive thinking is what leads to positive actions, actions that affect you and the people around you. When you think positively, your actions show how positive you are. You can create positive thinking by focusing on the good in life, even if it may feel tiny thing to feel happy about because when you once learn to be satisfied with minor things, you would think that you no longer feel the same amount of stress as before and now you would feel freer. This positive attitude will always find the good in everything, and life would seem much easier than before.

Being grateful for the things you have contributed a lot to your positive behavior. Gratitude has proven to reduce stress and improve self-esteem. Think of the things you are grateful for; for example, if someone gives you good advice, then be thankful to them, for if someone has helped you with something, then be grateful to them, by being grateful about minor things, you feel more optimistic about life, you feel that good things have always been coming to you. Studies show that making down a list of things you are grateful for during hard days helps you survive through the tough times.

A person laughing always looks like a happy person. Studies have shown that laughter lowers stress, anxiety, and depression. Open yourself up to humor, permit yourself to laugh even if forced because even a forced laugh can improve your mood. Laughter lightens the mood and makes problems seem more manageable. Your laughter is contagious, and it may even enhance the perspective of the people around us.

People with depression or anxiety are always their jailers; being harsh on themselves will only cause pain, negativity, and insecurity. So try to be soft with yourself, give yourself a positive talk regularly; it has proven to affect a person's actions. A positive word to yourself can influence your ability to regulate your feelings and thoughts. The positivity you carry in your brain is expressed through your actions, and who doesn't loves an optimistic person. Instead of blaming yourself, you can think differently, like "I will do better next time" or "I can fix this." Being optimistic about the complicated situation can lead your brain to find a solution to that problem.

When you wake up, it is good to do something positive in the morning, which mentally freshens you up. You can start the day by reading a positive quote about life and understand the meaning of that quote, and you may feel an overwhelming feeling after letting the meaning set. Everybody loves a good song, so start by listening to a piece of music that gives you positive vibes, that gives you hope, and motivation for the day. You can also share your positivity by being nice to someone or doing something nice for someone; you will find that you feel thrilled and positive by making someone else happy.

Surely you can't just start thinking positively in a night, but you can learn to approach things and people with a positive outlook with some practice.

Chapter 3:
6 Ways to Start All Over Again

If anyone tells you that you're meant to go from the crib to the running track, breeze through college, get your dream job, score the perfect partner, and live happily ever after all in one fell swoop, they're lying...and seriously delusional.

The reality is that life is anything but a straight line and is made up of seasons — some good, some mundane, and some so bad that you'll need plenty of time to recover from the trauma of living through it.

At your lowest point, you may think that your life is ruined and there's no way out.

But *listen* to me: **It WILL pass.** There's *always* a way forward. You just have to look for it. You can let the circumstances you're in ruin you, or you can allow it to improve you.

The process of rebuilding your life from the ground up won't be easy, but having a plan will greatly increase your chances of successfully carving out the life you want.

Here are my tried-and-tested steps to start with:

1. Start With Cleaning Up the Space You Live In
To build something good, you'll need good daily habits.

But to turn a new, unfamiliar (and therefore uncomfortable and 'quitable') action into a daily habit, you'll need to do everything you can to reduce the odds that you'll give up, particularly when you hit a speed bump.

One of the best ways to do this is to set up your environment for your success.

This means clearing the space where you spend the most time of clutter, trash, and chaos.

The result: A calmer, clearer, and focused mind that'll help you move forward with your plan and sticking to it.

2. Make Peace With Reality and Work With, Not Against It

We often get stuck in life because we're either unable or unwilling to accept our reality as it is. Instead, we stubbornly continue to indulge in fantasy, specifically, how we wish things were.

This is where you'll need to get real with yourself, no matter how unpleasant it is.

Ask yourself: What's your situation now, and how can you work with what is, not what you wish it was?

3. Reflect On What and Where You Went Wrong

No one starts out planning to fail or creating a disaster.

But somehow, we end up taking one or several wrong steps along the way and find ourselves on a painful path we never expected to be in.

Whether these missteps were driven by ego, a lack of awareness, miscalculation, denial, or simply carelessness, you owe it to yourself, to be honest with the captain of your ship: You.

It's only once you've taken the time to reflect and figure out what went wrong and where things started to fall apart that you can start putting together a new plan with your success-driving strategy baked in.

This is the plan that'll help you make the progress you've wanted all along.

4. Revisit Your Goals and Values

But wait.

Before you take one step forward on your new path, you'll need to make sure your foundation is solid.

You may have an idea of where you'd like to go: Run it through a stress test:

How do you want to live?

Does your idea align with your values?

What are your values anyway?

What will you do if someone close to you disagrees or tries to tear it down?

What will happen if you find yourself feeling tempted to stray away from it?

Put your ideas, values, and stress-test answers down on paper so you can see them all in one place and let them sink in.

5. Decide what you Want To Do Next

Now that you've some ideas for possible paths you could take that fall in line with your values, it's time to decide: Which one will you choose?

'Decision' comes from the Latin word decision, which means "to cut off."

But while picking one path means cutting yourself off from all others, it doesn't mean that you can't course-correct later on by choosing a different one if things don't work out or feel right.

6. Work Up The Courage To Do It

It's OK to feel terrified about heading into new, unchartered territory. It'd be weird if you didn't. But know that this is the point where you start putting one foot in front of the other regardless of how you feel or chicken out and retreat into your cave. It's time to get moving despite the paralyzing fear and soul-crushing doubt that are making your feet and heart feel like lead.

Chapter 4:
How to Stop Chasing New Goals All the Time

The philosopher Alan Watts always said that life is like a song, and the sole purpose of the song is to dance. He said that when we listen to a song, we don't dance to get to the end of the music. We dance to enjoy it. This isn't always how we live our lives. Instead, we rush through our moments, thinking there's always something better, there's always some goal we need to achieve.

"Existence is meant to be fun. It doesn't go anywhere; it just is." Our lives are not about things and status. Even though we've made ourselves miserable with wanting, we already have everything we need. Life is meant to be lived. If you can't quit your job tomorrow, enjoy where you are. Focus on the best parts of every day. Believe that everything you do has a purpose and a place in the world.

Happiness comes from gratitude. You're alive, you have people to miss when you go to work, and you get to see them smile every day. We all have to do things we don't want to do; we have to survive. When you find yourself working for things that don't matter, like a big house or a fancy car, when you could be living, you've missed the point. You're playing the song, but you're not dancing.

"A song isn't just the ending. It's not just the goal of finishing the song. The song is an experience."

We all think that everything should be amazing when we're at the top, but it's not. Your children have grown older, and you don't remember the little things.

"...tomorrow and plans for tomorrow can have no significance at all unless you are in full contact with the reality of the present since it is in the present and only in the present that you live."

You feel cheated of your time, cheated by time. Now you have to make up for it. You have to live, make the most of what you have left. So you set another goal.

This time you'll build memories and see places, do things you never got the chance to do. The list grows, and you wonder how you'll get it all done and still make your large mortgage payment. You work more hours so you can do all this stuff "someday." You've overwhelmed yourself again.

You're missing the point.

Stop wanting more, <u>be grateful for</u> today. Live in the moment. Cherish your life and the time you have in this world. If it happens, it happens. If it doesn't, then it wasn't meant to; let it go.

"We think if we don't interfere, it won't happen."

There's always an expectation, always something that has to get done. You pushed aside living so that you could live up to an expectation that doesn't exist to anyone but you. The expectation is always there because you gave it power. To live, you've got to let it go.

You save all your money so that you can retire. You live to retire. Then you get old, and you're too tired to live up to the expectation you had of retirement; you never realize your dreams.

At forty, you felt cheated; at eighty, you are cheated. You cheated yourself the whole way through to the end.

"Your purpose was to dance until the end, but you were so focused on the end that you forgot to dance."

Chapter 5:
Six Steps To Create A Vision For Your Life

Hi everyone, for today's video, we are going to talk about how to create life's visions. You might be thinking, "why do we need to make these visions?" or "what are these visions for?".

Let me ask you this question, have you ever felt so stuck in where you are? That feeling when you wanna move and be somewhere else because you don't like where you are but you don't know where to go either? That is the worst feeling ever, right?

Creating a vision for your life will save you from being stuck and lost. These visions are the pictures you create about the life that you want to live.

Here are 6 Steps To Start Envisioning Your Future

Step number 1, identify what matters to you. Ask yourself, "what's really important to me?". Is it health? Career? Wealth? Relationships? Passion?

Time? It could be a balance of all those things. What legacy would you want to leave in this world? Identifying what truly matters to you and what you really value gives you a destination of where you want to be. Having these in mind, all your plans and decisions will be centered towards your destination.

Next step is thinking ahead, but at the same time, also believing that it is already happening for you right now. Be specific in chasing what you want, don't just simply limit yourself to what you think is socially acceptable. If you limit your choices to what seems to be reasonable, you are disconnecting yourself from your true potentialDon't compromise.. Be as audacious as you want to be, it's your own life anyway! You have all the right to dream as big as you want. Talk as if your dreams are happening right now. When you have this big dream, you won't settle for less just because it is what's available at the moment.

Step number 3, assess and challenge your motives. Ask yourself, "is this the kind of life I wanna live because it is what the society is expecting from me?", "am I doing this because this is what everybody else is doing?" Knowing your real motive towards your visions will help you uncover what your heart really desires. You might even be surprised by what you'll discover within you when you remove all the layers that the world has planted in you.

Next step, be sure that your visions are aligned with a purpose. You don't need to know exactly what your life purpose is, unless you've already figured that out somehow. But your visions should be relevant to how you want your life to be. For example, if your goal is to maintain your mental well-being, your vision might be to live your life peacefully while focusing on the things that truly matter. Your vision should serve you the purpose into making your life as pleasing as you want it.

Step number 5 is to be accountable for your own visions. Don't tie your visions into someone else's hands. Your visions may involve direct impact to others but make sure that your visions are not dependent on other people. Why? Because people, just like the seasons, change. People come and go. The version of the people in your life right now is not how they will be for the rest of their lives. And so are you. Hold these visions in your own hands and make sure you execute it diligently and faithfully.

Last step is to make room for changes. You will grow as a person, that is a fact. You won't have the same exact priorities all through your life. And that's okay. Whatever you want to change into is valid. Your goals and dreams are all valid. Changes are inevitable so don't be afraid if you have to change what's working for you from time to time.

While you are in the process of making your life's visions, be as creative as you can. Although the world is not a wish-granting factory, remember that through your hard work and perseverance, nothing is really impossible. You have everything in you to achieve your goals and live through your visions. You just need to be clear about what you really want or where you wanna be.

Remember that our days in this world are limited. We won't be able to live our lives to the fullest if we are just merely existing or living by default. We are humans. And as humans, we have the power to lead the life we truly desire. Sometimes, we are just one decision away from it.

I hope what we've talked about today will not just inspire you to make your life's visions but also help you to understand why you need to make them. You deserve a kind of life that will excite you to wake up everyday because you know what you are waking up for.

Chapter 6:
Why You Should Master One Thing AT a time

Many people, myself included, have multiple areas of life they would like to improve. For example, I would like to reach more people with my writing, lift heavier weights at the gym, and practice mindfulness more consistently. Those are just a few of the goals I find desirable, and you probably have a long list yourself.

The problem is, even if we are committed to working hard on our goals, our natural tendency is to revert to our old habits at some point. Making a permanent lifestyle change is difficult.

What Happens When You Focus on One Thing

Here is another science-based reason to focus on one thing at a time:

When you begin practicing a new habit, it requires a lot of conscious effort to remember to do it. After a while, however, the pattern of behavior becomes easier. Eventually, your new habit becomes a normal routine, and the process is more or less mindless and automatic.

Researchers have a fancy term for this process called "automaticity." Automaticity is the ability to perform a behavior without thinking about each step, which allows the pattern to become automatic and habitual.

But here's the thing: automaticity only occurs as the result of lots of repetition and practice. The more reps you put in, the more automatic a behavior becomes.

That said, a study found the <u>average habit takes about 66 days to become automatic</u>. (Don't put too much stock in that number. The range in the study was very wide, and the only reasonable conclusion you should make is that it will take months for new habits to become sticky.)

Change Your Life Without Changing Your Entire Life

Alright, let's review what I have suggested to you so far and figure out some practical takeaways.

1. You are 2x to 3x more likely to follow through with a habit if you make a specific plan for when, where, and how you will implement it. This is known as an implementation intention.

2. You should focus entirely on one thing. Research has found that implementation intentions do not work if you try to improve multiple habits simultaneously.

3. Research has shown that any given habit becomes more automatic with more practice. On average, it takes at least two months for new habits to become automatic behaviors.

This brings us to the punchline of this article…

The counterintuitive insight from all of this research is that the best way to change your entire life is by not changing your entire life. Instead, it is best to focus on one specific habit, work on it until you master it, and make it an automatic part of your daily life. Then, repeat the process for the next habit.

The way to master more things, in the long run, is to simply focus on one thing right now.

Chapter 7:
Dealing with Career Pressure.

Dealing with pressure related to work is A very difficult thing to achieve. People deal with career-related pressures daily. Be it A job or A business or even studies. In the fast-evolving world of today, people often forget about their own mental and physical health because of the immense pressures of work and the environment. There are many things that you can do to lower this pressure and become more productive.

The first thing to do is to stay calm. This is not an easy thing to do but is very effective. Staying positive under pressure can help you to stay calm and complete the task at hand. To stay positive, A person should always be optimistic and should always believe that they can complete the task under pressure. The next goal is to stay focused on the task. One should always let go of thoughts that are getting in the way of their work and slowing them down. Staying focused helps you to achieve your goals before the deadline. This is one step closer to self-appreciation, which is very helpful in situations where the pressure is high. Another way of reducing pressure is to stay away from any arguments within the organization because getting engaged in them can lead to stress and wasting your own time.

On the other hand, if you are not engaging in arguments, your reputation within the organization can become better, and sometimes employees that are loyal to the organization get easier tasks as compared to employees that are causing trouble. Asking for help is always A way of reducing pressure. A task can be achieved much quicker if A bunch of people are working together. This is why workgroups are formed within an organization because they increase efficiency. Asking for help is never bad, and one must not be ashamed of doing so. Utilizing your holidays for your betterment can lead to reducing work-related pressure and stress. Lastly, people who rely on coffee and chocolate snacks should limit their intake because these are stimulants. Taking them in a small amount is fine, but drinking too much coffee or eating too much chocolate snacks can cause undue stress and restlessness, which can make the already stressful situation even worse.

There are A lot of seminars and activities to help you perform better under pressure. Joining them can be very beneficial for A person who is having difficulties in these areas. Choosing the right career for yourself is also better because if A person is doing what they enjoy, there is very little pressure because they are having A good time. On the other hand, if A person chooses A career that is not made for them, however good they are at it, A time will come when they will be questioning their decision, and they won't be able to do anything about it. Proper career counselling can be very helpful, and everyone should seek it before opting for A career. These experts evaluate A person and help them to choose the right career which they can perform better and be happy with their job. Finding A career that suits you best and working hard towards it will ensure your success. Getting pressured about choosing the right career is common, but as long as you are satisfied with what you choose, you are good to go!

Chapter 8:
6 Steps To Get Out of Your Comfort Zone

The year 2020 and 2021 have made a drastic change in all our lives, which might have its effect forever. The conditions of last year and a half have made a certain lifestyle choice for everyone, without having a say in it for us.

This new lifestyle has been a bit overwhelming for some and some started feeling lucky. Most of us feel comfortable working from home, and taking online classes while others want to have some access to public places like parks and restaurants.

But the pandemic has affected everyone more than once. And now we are all getting used to this relatively new experience of doing everything from home. Getting up every day to the same routine and the same environment sometimes takes us way back on our physical and mental development and creativity.

So one must learn to leave the comfort zone and keep themselves proactive. Here are some ways anyone can become more productive and efficient.

Everyone is always getting ready to change but never changing.

1. Remember your Teenage Self

People often feel nostalgic remembering those days of carelessness when they were kids and so oblivious in that teenage. But, little do they take for inspiration or motivation from those times. When you feel down, or when you don't feel like having the energy for something, just consider your teenage self at that time.

If only you were a teenager now, you won't be feeling lethargic or less motivated. Rather you'd be pushing harder and harder every second to get the job done as quickly as possible. If you could do it back then, you still can! All you need is some perspective and a medium to compare to.

2. Delegate or Mentor someone

Have you ever needed to have someone who could provide you some guidance or help with a problem that you have had for some time?

I'm sure, you weren't always a self-made man or a woman. Somewhere along the way, there was someone who gave you the golden quote that changed you consciously or subconsciously.

Now is the time for you to do the same for someone else. You could be a teacher, a speaker, or even a mentor who doesn't have any favors to ask in return. Once you get the real taste of soothing someone else's pain, you won't hesitate the next time.

This feeling of righteousness creates a chain reaction that always pushes you to get up and do good for anyone who could need you.

3. Volunteer in groups

The work of volunteering may seem pointless or philanthropic. But the purpose for you to do it should be the respect that you might get, but the stride to get up on your feet and help others to be better off.

Volunteering for flood victims, earthquake affectees or the starving people of deserts and alpines can help you understand the better purpose of your existence. This keeps the engine of life running.

4. Try New Things for a Change

Remember the time in Pre-school when your teachers got you to try drawing, singing, acting, sculpting, sketching, and costume parties. Those weren't some childish approach to keep you engaged, but a planned system to get your real talents and skills to come out.

We are never too old to learn something new. Our passions are unlimited just as our dreams are. We only need a push to keep discovering the new horizons of our creative selves.

New things lead to new people who lead to new places which might lead to new possibilities. This is the circle of life and life is ironic enough to rarely repeat the same thing again.

You never know which stone might lead you to a gold mine. So never stop discovering and experiencing because this is what makes us the supreme being.

5. Push Your Physical Limits

This may sound cliched, but it always is the most important point of them all. You can never get out of your comfort zone, till you see the world through the hard glass.

The world is always softer on one side, but the image on the other side is far from reality. You can't expect to get paid equally to the person who works 12 hours a day in a large office of hundreds of employees. Only if you have the luxury of being the boss of the office.

You must push yourself to search for opportunities at every corner. Life has always more and better to offer at each stop, you just have to choose a stop.

6. Face Your Fears Once and For All

People seem to have a list of Dos and Dont's. The latter part is mostly because of a fear or a vacant thought that it might lead to failure for several reasons.

You need a "Do it all" behavior in life to have an optimistic approach to everything that comes in your way.

What is the biggest most horrible thing that can happen if you do any one of these things on your list? You need to have a clear vision of the possible worst outcome.

If you have a clear image of what you might lose, now must try to go for that thing and remove your fear once and for all. Unless you have something as important as your life to lose, you have nothing to fear from anything.

No one can force you to directly go skydiving if you are scared of heights. But you can start with baby steps, and then, maybe, later on in life you dare to take a leap of faith.

"Life is a rainbow, you might like one color and hate the other. But that doesn't make it ugly, only less tempting".

All you need is to be patient and content with what you have today, here, right now. But, you should never stop aiming for more. And you certainly shouldn't regret it if you can't have or don't have it now.

People try to find their week spots and frown upon those moments of hard luck. What they don't realize is, that the time they wasted crying for what is in the past, could have been well spent for a far better future they could cherish for generations to come.

Chapter 9:
10 Habits of Emma Stone

Emma Stone, an Academy Award-winning actress made her debut in 2007 with the teen comedy "Superbad." Since then, she has become one of the most demanded actress of her time, amassing honours, nominations and captivating audiences on and off the big screen with her effortless, pleasant acting style and her attitude.

Stone's wide eyes and seemingly effortless brilliance shine through in practically every job she lands, making her one of the most renowned movies star. But, even if you've seen every one of Stone's films, there are likely a few facts you don't know about this extraordinary actress.

Here are 10 habits of Emma Stone that can be yours too.

1. Be Your Worst Judgement

According to Emma Stone, being your worst critique push you to work hard on yourself because your set standards are high. As long as you're true to yourself, what others think is not a concern. It's not about being cruel to oneself but about pushing yourself to new heights.

2. Understand Your Interests

Emma presented a PowerPoint presentation of her work to her parents for review. That earned her permission to relocate to Los Angeles in 2004 to pursue her acting career. She knew exactly what she wanted because it was her passion, and she didn't let anyone get in her way. You know you're enthusiastic about something when you're willing to go to any length to make it happen.

3. A Clear Vision

Stone is always quite clear about what she wants out of life. She does not allow short-term distractions or anything else to get in her way. She feels that the key to success is first to decide exactly what you want. The more precise your concept, the easier it will be to make it come to life.

4. Perseverance

Emma stone's route to Success, for example, her character Mia in La La La Land, was never an easy one. After she moved to California, she tried several roles, which was until 2007 she gained widespread notoriety for her appearance in the comedy "Superbad."
It took her five years have her first taste of success in acting. That kind of perseverance keeps her striving for the best, and so can you.

5. Education Equates No Worth

Stone has didn't allow societal assumptions and stigma to limit her. She made her acting debut when she was 11 years old. At the age of 15, she decided to drop out of high school and to pursue her acting career. In a world full of standardized tests, it is normal for people to assess you based on your educational level or even link it to your level of Success.

6. Eat that Dang Red Velvet Cupcake

The world is your oyster, and life is brief. So live your life, and don't allow anything to stop you from making the most of it.

7. No Barriers You Can't Conquer

Emma Stone revealed that she suffered from anxiety and panic attacks as a child. She opted for treatment and performance to help her get over it and keep chasing her aspirations. When you face challenges in your life, giving up is like giving up on the critical part of yourself. Losing faith in yourself means that your aspirations and passions are put on hold.

8. Do What Brings You Joy

If you are dissatisfied with your current circumstances, you must make a change. Life is too short to spend it doing things that make you miserable or even melancholy. For Emma, this means that you should treat yourself now and then, especially on bad days. Cherish the little things in life.

9. Look Up to Your Role Models

Emma broke down in tears when Mel B spoke to her through a video message. Of course, you don't have to cry when you meet your role model. But it's magnificent to have someone to look up to, that strong person who gives you strength on bad days.

10. Don't Over Plan

Having a precise aim and knowing where you want to go in life is absolutely a positive thing. But don't over plan because life might take an unexpected turn at any time. Emma, in an interview, said that she is a person who will never make a five-year plan and that she only depends on her intuition. Follow your intuition, and if it's correct, things will fall into place.

Conclusion

As Emma did, live your life, and don't allow anything to stop you from making the most of it.

Chapter 10:
5 Tips to Doing Unique and Meaningful Work

When you think about meaningful work, you think about Mother Theresa or Princess Diana or maybe Peace Corp workers or school teachers and nurses. All of these are great and meaningful jobs. But, not everyone can raise money and attention to help get landmines cleared, nor can (or should) everyone try to teach second grade. And if blood makes you faint, nursing isn't a great idea for you either.

So, how can you make your job meaningful work, even when it's not directly making anyone's life better? These five suggestions will change your job from tedious work to meaningful work.

1. Look at the Big Picture

Why does your job exist? You could be an HR manager, a grocery store cashier, or a tech company CEO. Each of these jobs is necessary to make the world a better place.

Because this is no longer an agrarian society, you need the grocery store cashier to get food. CEOs of well-managed companies provide goods and services to the community and jobs with paychecks for many people. And HR managers can make people's lives much better by helping them progress in their careers, finding and providing the best benefits, and hiring great people.

If you just look at the tasks in front of you, you'll forget how you contribute to the community as a whole.

2. Treat Each Other With Kindness

A kind person can change everyone's day from drudgery to fun. Yes, work is still working, and sometimes it's hard, but working with the right people can make you look forward to working even if the job is hard work.

One man who worked for a brewery as a delivery man could have seen his job as hard work and struggle. After all, his job duty was to drive from restaurant to restaurant, carrying huge kegs of beer and taking out the old, empty ones. But, the people in many restaurants cheered when the beer guy came in with the beer kegs. Their act of kindness changed his job from drudgery to one that he loved.

3. Work Hard

How does working hard make a job meaningful? Well, hard work often equals success. When you succeed in your job, you help others in your department succeed in their jobs. When your whole department succeeds, the company succeeds. That is pretty meaningful.

Additionally, hard work is easier than avoiding work. Think about it: when you have to worry if your boss knows how much time you're spending surfing the internet, that adds another layer of complexity to your job. When you're working hard all of the time, and your boss drops by, it's not a big deal.

When you keep on top of your work, you have lowered stress levels. Now, of course, some people are overburdened and cannot accomplish everything. You might start feeling like, "I can't get everything done, so why bother?" These feelings of stress and failure can pose a huge temptation, but don't give in. First of all, you'll start to feel like your job just isn't meaningful—it's just work. Second, that adds additional stress on top of your head.

What you do instead is go to your boss and say directly, "I have five tasks on my plate right now. I can do four effectively, or I can do a lousy job on all five. Which would you prefer?" or "I have five tasks on my plate right now. I only have time to get three of them done. Which two should I skip?"

4. Look Outside of Your Job

Does your meaningful work have to be your day job? Of course not. Sometimes your day job can fund your meaningful work. Work-life balance means having a life. Whether it's through your family, church, charity, art, or whatever is important to you, you need a paycheck to support that.

You don't have to fulfill all of your needs through your paid job. You don't even need to feel guilty that you're working for a large corporation rather than a small non-profit. It's not bad to earn money. You find your meaning in how you can spend that money.

5. Consider Changing Jobs

If you just can't see how your current job is meaningful, and you can't figure out a way to make your job meaningful work, then perhaps it's time for you to move on. If your job doesn't bring you joy, doesn't allow you to support your family or essential charitable causes, and doesn't help the community, then maybe it's not the right job for you.

No one has a skill set that is so tiny and unique that there is only one job in the world that would suit them. And if you have no marketable skills, get training in new skills. You don't have to invest in a college degree if that's not your goal.

Chapter 11:

Believe in Yourself

Listen up. I want to tell you a story. This story is about a boy. A boy who became a man, despite all odds. You see, when he was a child, he didn't have a lot going for him. The smallest and weakest in his class, he had to struggle every day just to keep up with his peers. Every minute of every hour was a fight against an opponent bigger and stronger than he was - and every day he was knocked down. Beaten. Defeated. But... despite that... despite everything that was going against him... this small, weak boy had one thing that separated him from hundreds of millions of people in this world. A differentiating factor that made a difference in the matter of what makes a winner in this world of losers. You see this boy believed in himself. No matter the odds, he believed fundamentally that he had the power to overcome anything that got in his way! It didn't matter how many times he was knocked down, he got RIGHT BACK UP!

Now it wasn't easy. It hurt like hell. Every time he failed was another reminder of how far behind he was. A reminder of the nearly insurmountable gap between him and everyone else and lurking behind that reminder was the temptation, the suggestion to just give up. Throw in the towel. Surrender the win. Yet believe me when I tell you that no matter HOW tough things got, no matter HOW much he wanted to give in, a small voice in his heart keep saying... not today... just once more... I know it hurts but I can try again... Just. Once. More.

You see more than anything in this world HE KNEW that deep inside him was a greatness just WAITING to be tapped into! A power that most people would never see, but not him. It didn't matter what the world threw at him, because he'd be damned if he let his potential die alongside him. And all it took? All it required to unlock the chasm of greatness inside was a moment to realise the lies the world tried to tell him. In less than a second he recognised the light inside that would ignite a spark of success to address the ones who didn't believe that he could do it. The ones who told him to give up! Get out! Go home and roam the streets where failure meets those who weren't born to sit at the seat at the top!

Yet what they didn't know is that being born weak didn't matter any longer 'cause in his fight to succeed he became stronger. Rising up to the heights beyond, he WOULD NOT GIVE UP till he forged a bond within his heart that ensured NO MATTER THE ODDS, no matter what anyone said about him, no matter what the world told him, he had something that NO ONE could take away from him. A power so strong it transformed this boy into a man. A loser into a winner. A failure into a success. That, is the power of self-belief...

Chapter 12:
Five Steps to Clarify Your Goals

Today, we're going to talk about how and why you should start clarifying your goals.

But first, let me ask you, why do you think setting clear goals is important?

Well, imagine yourself running at a really fast speed, but you don't know where you're going. You just keep running and running towards any direction without a destination in mind. What do you think will happen next? You'll be exhausted. But will you feel fulfilled? Not really. Why? Because despite running at breakneck speed and being busy, you have failed to identify an end point. Without it, you won't know how far or near you are to where you are supposed to be. The same analogy applies to how we live our lives. No matter how productive you are or how fast your pacing is, at the end the race, if you don't have clear goals, you will simply end up wondering what the whole point of running was in the first place. You might end up in a place that you didn't intend to be. Neglecting the things that are most important on you, while focusing on all the wrong things- and that is not the best way to live your life.

So, how can we change that? How can we clarify our goals so that we are sure that we are running the race we intended to all along?

1. Imagine The Ideal Version of Yourself

Try to picture the kind of person you want to be. The things you want to have. The people you want around you. The kind of life that your ideal self is living. How does your ideal-self make small and big decisions? How does he or she perceive the world? Don't limit your imagination to what you think is pleasant and acceptable in society.

Fully integrate that ideal image of yourself into your subconscious mind and see yourself filling those shoes. That is the only way that you'll be able to see it as a real person.

Remember that the best version of yourself doesn't need to be perfect. But this is your future life so dream as big as you want, and genuinely believe that you'll be able to become that person someday in the near future.

2. Identify The Gap Between Your Ideal and Present Self

Take a hard look at your current situation now and ask yourself honesty: "How far am I away now from the person I know I need to become one day? What am I lacking at present that I am not doing or acting upon? Are there any areas that I can identify that I need to work on? Are there any new habits that I need to adopt to become that person?

Be unbiased in your self-assessment as that is the only way to give yourself a clear view of knowing exactly what you need to start working on today. Be brutally honest with your self-evaluation.

It is okay to be starting from scratch if that is where are at this point. Don't be afraid of the challenge, instead embrace and prepare yourself for the journey of a lifetime. It is way worse not knowing when and where to begin than starting from nothing at all.

3. Start Making Your Action Plan

Once you have successfully identified the gap between your present self and your ideal self, start to list down all the actions you need to take and the things that need to be done. Breakdown your action plan into milestones. Make it specific, measurable and realistic. If your action plans don't work the way you think they will, don't be afraid to make new plans. Remember that your failed plans are just part of the whole journey so enjoy every moment of it. Don't be hard on yourself while you're in the process. You're a human and not a machine. Don't forget to rest and recharge from time to time. You will be more inspired and will have more energy to go through your action plan if you are taking care of yourself at the same time.

4. Set A Timeline

Now that you have identified your overarching goal and objectives, set a period of time when you think it is reasonable for a certain milestone to be completed. You don't need to be so rigid with this timeline. Instead use it as sort of a guiding light. This guide is to serve as a reminder to provide a sense of urgency to work on your goals consistently. Don't beat yourself up unnecessarily if you do not meet your milestones as you have set up. Things change and problems do come up in our lives. As long as you keep going, you're perfectly fine. Remember that it is not about how slow or how fast you get to your destination, it is about how you persevere to continue your journey.

5. Aim For Progress, Not Perfection

You are living in an imperfect world with an imperfect system. Things will never be perfect but it doesn't mean that it will be less beautiful. While you're in the process of making new goals and working on them as you go along, always make room for mistakes and adjustments. You can plan as much as you want but life has its own way of doing things. When unforeseen events take place, don't be afraid to make changes and adjustments, or start over if you must. Even though things will not always go the way you want them to, you can still be in control of choosing how you'll move forward.

As humans, we never want to be stuck. We always want to be somewhere better. But sometimes, we get lost along the way. If we have a clear picture of where we want to be, no matter how many detours we encounter, we'll always find our way to get to our destination. And you know what, sometimes those detours are what we exactly need to keep going through our journey.

Chapter 13:
Consistency can bring you happiness.

Happiness is an individual concept.

One man's riches is another man's rubbish.

As humans we are not happy if we do not have a routine, a reason to get up, and a purpose to live.

Without working towards something consistently, we become lost.

We begin to drift.

Drifting with no purpose eventually leads to emptiness.

When we are drifting in a job we hate,

We are trading our future away,

When we inconsistent in our relationships,

Problems are bound to arise.

Choose consistent focus instead.

Figure out exactly what you want and start to change it.

Employ consistent routines and habits that to move you towards your goals.

Consistency and persistence are key to success and happiness.

Without consistent disciplined effort towards what we want, we resign to a life of mediocrity.

Read a book for an hour consistently every single day.
You will become a national expert in 1 year.
In 5 years, a global expert.
That is the power of consistency.
Instead, people spend most of their free time scrolling through social media.

Consistency starts in the mind.
Control your thoughts to be positive despite the circumstances.
Nothing in the world can make us happy if we choose not to be.

Choose to be happy now and consistently working towards your goals.
We cannot be happy and successful if we dwell in the day to day setbacks.

We must consistently move like a bulldozer.
We have to keep going no matter what.
Nothing stays in the path of a bulldozer for too long.

In life, no matter where you are, you only ever have two choices.
Choose to stay where you are? Or choose to keep moving?

If where you are is making you happy, then by all means do more of it.
If not. What will? And why?
This should be clear before you take action.
Start with the end in your mind.
Let your body catch-up to it afterwards.

The end result is your what.
The action required is your how.
Concentrate on the what and the how and it will all be revealed soon enough.

Concentrate consistently on what you want for yourself and your family.
Distraction and lack of consistent action is a killer of happiness and success.
Your happiness is the life you want.
Take consistent action towards that life you've always dreamed of.
Commitment and endurance is part of that process.

On earth things need time to nurture and grow.
Everything in life depends on it.
The right conditions for maximum growth.

You can't just throw a seed on the concrete and expect it to grow with no soil and water,
Just as you can't simply wish for change and not create the right environment for success.

A seed requires not just consistent sunlight,
But the perfect combination of water and nutrients as well.
You might have given that seed sunlight,
just as you have your dream hope,
But without faith and consistent action towards the goal, nothing will happen.

The seed will still stay a seed forever.

Consistency in thought and action is everything towards happiness.
Nothing can grow without it.
Your success can be measured by your time spent working towards your goals.
If we consistently do nothing we become successful in nothing.
If we have to do something, should it not be something worth doing?

Start doing things that make you happy and fulfilled.
Consistency towards something that makes you happy is key towards lasting success.
Adapt when necessary but remain consistent with the end result in mind.
The path can be changed when necessary but the destination cannot.
Accepting anything less is admitting defeat.

Consistent concentration on the end result can and will be tested.
It however cannot be defeated, unless you quit.
If we remain steadfast in our belief that this is possible for us, it will be possible.
After a while things will seem probable. Eventually it becomes definite.

Continue to believe you can do it despite the circumstances.
Continue despite everyone around you saying you can't do it.

In spite of social status,
in spite of illness or disability,

in spite of age, race or nationality,

know you can do nearly anything if you consistently put all of your mind and body towards the task.

Take the pressure off.

There is no set guideline.

It is what you make of it.

There is no set destination or requirements.

Those are set my you.

The only competition is yourself from yesterday.

If you can consistently outperform that person, your success is guaranteed.

Consistent concentration and action towards your dream is key you your success and happiness.

Chapter 14:
Why You're Demotivated By A Values Conflict

Every human being, in fact, every organism in this universe is different from even the same member of their species. Every one of us has different traits, likes, dislikes, colors, smells, interests so it's natural to have a difference of opinion.

It's natural to have a different point of view. It's natural and normal to have a different way of understanding. And it's definitely normal for someone else to disagree with your ways of dealing with things.

Most of us don't want to see someone disagreeing with us because we have this tricky little fellow inside of us that we call EGO.

Our ego makes us feel disappointed when we see or hear someone doing or saying something better than us. We cannot let go of the fact that someone might be right or that someone might be Okay with being wrong and we can't do a single thing about it.

This conflict of values occurs within ourselves as well. We want to do one thing but we cannot leave the other thing as well. We want to have something but we cannot keep it just because we don't have the resources to maintain them.

This feeling of 'want to have but cannot have' makes us susceptible to feelings of incompleteness ultimately making us depressed. The reality of life is that you can't always get what you want. But that doesn't make it a good enough reason to give up on your dreams or stop thinking about other things too.

Life has a lot to offer to us. So what if you can't have this one thing you wanted the most. Maybe it wasn't meant for you in the first place. Nature has a way of giving you blessings even when you feel like you have nothing.

Let's say you want something but your mind tells you that you can't have it. So what you should do is to find alternative ways to go around your original process of achieving that thing and wait for new results. What you should do is to give up on the idea altogether just because you have a conflict within your personality.

You cannot let this conflict that is building within you get a hold of you. Clear your mind, remove all doubts, get rid of all your fears of failure or rejection, and start working from a new angle with a new perspective. Set new goals and new gains from the same thing you wanted the first time. This time you might get it just because you already thought you had nothing to lose.

This feeling of 'No Regret' will eventually help you get over any situation you ever come across after a fight with your inner self. This feeling can help you flourish in any environment no matter what other people say or do behind your back.

Nothing can bring you peace but yourself. Nothing holds you back but your other half within you.

Chapter 15:
It's Not Your Job to Tell Yourself "No"

How many times have you had the chance to go around something that could have changed your life? What were your thoughts when you decided to enter a state where even the slightest thought of failure leads you to stop acting on it?

I'm sure every one of us has a good reason behind everything we opt to do or don't in our lives.

But there is never a good enough reason to back down just because we have some examples of failures on our hands.

No one can decide what reality and nature have decided for them. Everyone must learn to juggle life and play with every piece they get a hand on.

Everything in life is meant to be taken as a risk. You can never learn to swim till you get your first dive in a deep pool. You never learn to ride a bike till you have no one behind you to stop you from falling.

Everyone needs a bump every now and then. And when you finally decide to hike that hurdle, you finally start to see the horizon.

We all seem to get depressed more easily than we start to get motivated. We seem to get carried away with every stone that life throws back at us but we never try to catch that stone. We never try to indulge in one more suffering just to get better at what we are tested with.

Nobody wants to fail and that's why no one wants to take a chance at what might fail.

The mere fear of facing failure makes us build a mechanism of self-defense that forces us to say 'No' to anything that might hurt us one day.

But the reality is that it is illogical to stop just so you are afraid to face the reality. The reality is that you are a sane human and this is life. Life tests us in ways hardly imaginable.

When you say 'No' to yourself, it rarely means 'Not Now'. It always means 'Maybe some other time'. But deep down we already know that we will never attempt to do that thing. At least not consciously.

We always try for the best. We try to be the best at what we already have and are already doing. We are motivated enough to try new things, things that are more scary and unknown to us.

What we really should be doing is to try and get a taste of newer victories. Trying to search for new horizons. Trying to get what most fail to achieve. Because every other man or woman is just like us, afraid to fail and avoiding embarrassment. Our embarrassments are mostly self-imposed and we are the better judge of our failures.

There is no motivation and inspiration more powerful in the world than the spark that ignites within you.

Our sole purpose in life is to embrace everything that we come across. It is never to prevent something just because you don't have the courage to face your failures yet.

Chapter 16:
Dealing with Difficult Bosses.

Sometimes bosses can be A bit difficult to handle because of their expectations and behavior with the employees. But they are not impossible to deal with. You should never be discouraged by their behavior. Some people resign because of this, but in the end, the boss is not the one who is affected by this bold step, but the employee who takes this decision is affected because finding A rewarding job is never easy. There are ways to deal with difficult bosses, and by doing so, an employee can achieve big things and, at the same time, learn how to work in this environment.

The first and foremost thing to do is to evaluate the aspect because of which the boss is being difficult to work for. After that, think of the stuff that can be done to tackle that aspect. Even difficult bosses are good when you give them good results. They can be very rewarding because their expectations are always very high, so if an employee performs according to their expectations, they reward that employee generously. Some bosses get annoyed when employees skip the office or are late for work. Even in situations like illness, they are reluctant to give days off. If your boss is like this, the only thing to do is reduce your chances of illness. If A boss is target-oriented, you should be very focused on your task and should try to complete it before time to eliminate any chance of trouble. The next solution is not to be associated with groups that always cause trouble for the organization. Bosses can give A very tough time to employees who delay the targets by causing unwanted trouble.

To get the boss' attention, you should be on good terms with the managers because they are the ones who report to the leader, so by being on good terms with the managers, they will speak highly of you with the boss, and he will be happy by our attitude which can reduce the chances of behavioral problems by the boss. Increasing productivity is the key to being in the good books of A boss. In the end, it all comes to profitability which leaders care about the most. So if you are A good asset to the organization, the boss will hardly ever bother you. Also, when in direct communication with the boss, an employee should be in A very presentable manner, not only in terms of clothing but also in terms of body language and presentation skills. Words should be chosen very carefully in front of bosses. Having good communication and presenting skills is the key to getting the boss' attention in A positive way.

Some bosses are indeed difficult to work for, but by following some basic rules of thumb, employees can work without the worry of the boss being annoyed. The key is to anticipate what the leader wants from his employees, and then it comes to meeting their expectations. Employees that prove to be A valuable asset for the organization are always rewarded by the leader because such employees are the reason for the organization's success. A company can be successful only if the boss and employees are willing to work together. Even if the boss is getting on your nerves, try not to let it get to you. Recognize your importance and work hard for your own sake.

Chapter 17:
NOTHING IS IMPOSSIBLE

Success is a concept as individual as beauty is, in the eye of the beholder, but with each individuals success comes testing circumstances, the price that must be paid in advance.

The grind,

The pain and the losses all champions have endured.

These hardships are no reason to quit but an indicator that you are heading in the right direction, because we must walk through the rain to see the rainbow and we must endure loss to make space for our new desired results.

Often the bigger the desired change , the bigger the pain, and this is why so few do it.

The very fact that are listening to this right now says to me you have something extra about you.

Inside you know there is more for you and that dream you have, you believe it is possible.

If others have done it before, then so can you , because we can do anything we set our minds and hearts to.

But we must take control of our destiny, have clear results in mind and take calculated action towards those results.

The path may be foggy and unknown but as you commit to the result and believe in it the path, it will be revealed soon enough.

We don't need to know the how, to declare we are going to do something, the how will come later.

Clear commitment to the result is key .

Too many people never live their dreams because they don't know how.

The how can be found out always if we can commit and believe fully in the process.

Faith is the magic elixir to success, without it nothing is possible.

What you believe about you is everything

If you believe you cannot swim and your dream is to be an Olympic swimming champion, what are your chances?

Any rational person would say, well learn to swim,

How many of you want to be multi-millionaires?

I guess everyone?

How many out there know how to get to such a status?

Would we just give up and say it is impossible?

Or would it be as logical as simply learning how to swim or ride a bike?

We believe someone could be an Olympic swimming champion with training and practice , but not a multi millionaire?

Many of us think big goals are simply too unrealistic.

Fear of failure , fear of what people might think , fear of change , all common reasons for aiming low in life.

But when we aim low and succeed the disappointment in that success is a foul tasting medicine.

Start gaining clarity in the reality of our results.

By thinking bigger we all have the ability to hit what seem now like unrealistic heights, but later realise that nothing is impossible.

We should all start from the assumption that we can do anything, it might take years of training but we can do it. Anything we set our minds to, we can do it.

So ask yourself right now those very important questions.

What exactly would I be doing right now that will make me the happiest person in the world? How much money do I want ?

What kind of relationships do I want?

When You have defined those things clearly,

Set the bar high and accept nothing less.

Because life will pay you any price.

But the time is ticking, you can't have it twice.

Chapter 18:
7 Ways To Develop Effective Communication With Your Clients

Effective communication is a significant factor in business; it is the essence of your business as clients are the core of every business. Sometimes, we forget what the client wanted; if this has happened to you, then you that your communication skills need a tad bit of improvement. The relationships you build with your clients are the key. Gaining loyal customers is essential, as they buy from you repeatedly and refer you to others, which increases customers. Communication can take many shapes and forms; it can be formal or informal and can happen over various platforms. Here are seven ways to develop practical communication skills with your clients.

1. **Make It About Your Clients**

When you meet someone that requires your services, you need to make it about them. It would help if you indeed gained your client's trust, but that doesn't mean the client has to hear your whole life story or several awards you have won. So whenever a new client seeks out help, remember that it is them that need help and focus on how you can impress them and meet their requirements. It is the best way to demonstrate your experience and extensive knowledge about the subject.

2. Treat Them How You'd Like To Be Treated

Business can be very tiring, sometimes when the stress is overbearing, we might feel moody and irritated but try not to take out the irritation on the clients, as your business exists because of your clients, so being rude with them will not be very wise. Try to be more patient, friendly, and positive with them, and your positive behavior shows your eagerness for your work. So try to treat your customers the most excellent way possible, the way you would want to be treated.

3. Respect Your Client's Time

"Time is money" we all have heard this famous saying, but what does it mean? The sentence gives away its meaning. It means that time is precious, whether it's yours or your clients'. Hence, try to avoid talking too much or wasting their time. Try not to make them wait for you too much that may cause unhealthiness in your relationship with your client. Try to get to the point without sounding rude or being blunt, be concise. Over media platforms, a short and well-planned consultation probably will do the work, and if they need any more information, they would ask you.

4. Listen To Your Clients

We all have met that annoying salesman that doesn't understand what you want or doesn't let you finish. If you have met someone like that, you know how irritating it could be, so when it is your time to be a businessman, don't do the same. When talking to your clients, please give them your undivided attention; you could do that by clearing up your brain of everything, no matter how busy the day is and how long the to-do list is. Take notes if you think you need them; try not to interrupt and stay silent if you think the customer wants to add a few more points. Listen actively to the client so that you can provide better customer service.

5. **Pay Attention To What Your Clients Say**

Any relationship requires attention; without attention, a client may seem very happy, and your business might not flourish the way you want it to. So pay attention to the tiniest of details of what the clients say. Take notes of the information that is hard to remember or seems essential. Ensure that you respond to emails, requests, or questions about your business; it will make the clients feel important. When sending out an email to your clients, double-check and see if you had made any mistakes, grammar mistakes indicate carelessness, and what kind of a client would want a careless person to help them.

6. **Actively Build Your Client Communication Skills**

If you want to create a lasting relationship with your customers, focus on your communication skills; you could set up a few rules and principles for yourself and your team to follow—brief your team on how to be friendly and provide the customer service required by the client. You can ask your client for their feedback on customer service; if they share something they don't like, you and your team can together work on that. Also, use client communication tools and software.

7. **Keep Records of Your Interactions**

Always keep records of your previous conversations with your clients; if you forgot a minor detail that was not so minor for them, it might not end pleasantly. Even the people who give clients their undivided attention forget things. So you could keep records of your interactions with your clients by making notes on a file or your mobile phone or by recording the conversation after they allow you. Making notes will also help you later, as it will help you remember who you need to check up on or follow up with.

Conclusion

Try to follow these ways, and win the trust of your clients. Be friendly and pleasant, and your clients will stay happy with you.

Chapter 19:

Stop Lying To Yourself

What do you think you are doing with your life? What do you keep on telling everyone you are up to? What ambitions do you make for yourself? What ideas do you follow? What goals do you want to follow and do you really have no choice in any of these?

These are not some random rude questions one might ask you. Because you deserve all of them if you still don't have anything meaningful in your life to stand behind.

You need to find a real achievement in your life that can make you feel accomplished.

Life is always a hard race to finish line with all of us running for the same goal of glory and success. But not all of us have the thing that will get us to that line first. SO when we fail to get there, we make reasons for our failure.

The reality is that it is never OK to make excuses for your failure when you weren't even eligible to join others to start with.

You have been lying to yourself this whole time, telling yourself that you have everything that takes to beat everyone to that finish line!

You have been lying to yourself saying that you are better than anyone there who came well prepared!

You keep telling yourself that you have a better understanding of things that you have just seen in your life for the first time! That you have a better approach towards life. That you know the best way to solve any problem.

Well, guess what my friend, You are wrong!

You don't have it all in you, you never did and you would probably never will. Because no man can master even one craft, let alone every. You need to do your homework for everything in your life, you try to master everything you come across but you can never really do so because you are a human. It is humanly impossible to be perfect at everything.

So stop calling yourself a saint or a self-taught genius because you are not.

You have this habit of lying to yourself because you find an escape from your faults. You find a way to cope with your inabilities. You find a way to soothe yourself that you are not wrong, just because everyone else says so.

You have to understand the fact that life has a way to be lived, and it is never the way of denial. It is rather the hopeful and quiet way of living your life with hard work and freedom.

You have to make your life worth living for. Because you know it in the back of your head that you have done the necessary hard work before to be able to compete among the best of the best out there.

You must have a strong feeling of justice towards yourself and towards others that makes you feel deserving of the highest honors and the biggest riches. Because you worked your whole life to be able to stand here and be a nominee for what life has to offer the best

Chapter 20:
How Successful People Figure What To Focus On

Peak performance experts say things like, "You should focus. You need to eliminate the distractions. Commit to one thing and become great at that thing."

This is good advice. The more I study successful people from all walks of life—artists, athletes, entrepreneurs, scientists—the more I believe focus is a core factor of success. But there is a problem with this advice too.

Of the many options in front of you, how do you know what to focus on? How do you know where to direct your energy and attention? How do you determine the *one thing* that you should commit to doing? I don't claim to have all the answers, but let me share what I've learned so far.

MAKE A CALL ABOUT WHAT TO FOCUS ON

Assuming you're willing to try things and experiment a bit, the next question is, "How do I know what's coming easily to me?"

The best answer I can give is to pay attention. Usually, this means measuring something.

- If you're an entrepreneur, track your marketing and promotion efforts.
- If you're trying to gain muscle, track your workouts.
- If you're learning an instrument, track your practice sessions.

Even when you do measure things, however, there comes the point where you have to make a call and decide what to focus on.

In my mind, this moment of decision is one of the central tensions of entrepreneurship. Do we continue trying new things, or do we double down on one strategy? Do we try to innovate, or do we commit to doing one thing well?

Everyone wants to know the right time to simplify and focus on one thing, but nobody does. That's what makes success so hard. Entrepreneurship isn't like baking a cake. There is no recipe. There is no guidebook.

At this stage, your best option is to decide. You can't try everything. At some point, you don't need more information, and you just need to make a choice.

Now we have reached the stage where figuring out what to focus on becomes a real possibility. Welcome to the grind. It's time to put in a volume of work. Not just once or twice. Not just when it's easy. But a consistent, repeated volume of work. You have to fall in love with boredom and stay on the bus.

It is through this sheer number of repetitions that you'll come to understand the fundamentals of your task. You might know what greatness looks like before this point, but you won't understand how to achieve greatness until you've put the work in yourself.

GETTING TO SIMPLE

Now, finally, after trying many things and figuring out what to focus on, and putting in enough reps, you can begin to simplify. You can trim away the fat because you know what is essential and what is unnecessary.

As the Frenchman Blaise Pascal famously wrote in his Provincial Letters, "If I had more time, I would have written you a shorter letter."

Mastering the fundamentals is often the hardest and longest journey of all.

Chapter 21:
HOW TO AVOID BURNOUT

Stress may be unavoidable, but burnout is preventable. Following these steps may help you thwart stress from getting the best of you:

Exercise

Not only is exercise good for our physical health, but it can also give us an emotional boost.

Stretched for time? You don't need to spend hours at the gym to reap these benefits. Mini-workouts and short walks are convenient ways to make exercise a daily habit.

Eat A Balanced Diet

Eating a healthy diet filled with omega-3 fatty acids can be a natural antidepressant. Adding foods rich in omega-3s like flaxseed oil, walnuts, and fish may help give your mood a boost.

Practice Good Sleep Habits

Our bodies need time to rest and reset, which is why healthy sleep habits are essential for our well-being.

Avoiding caffeine before bedtime, establishing a relaxing bedtime ritual, and banning smartphones from the bedroom can help promote sound sleep hygiene.

Ask For Help

During stressful times, it's important to reach out for help. If asking for assistance feels difficult, consider developing a self-ca6re "check-in" with close friends and family members so that you can take care of each other during trying times.

How To Help Friends Or Family Members

How can you help someone experiencing burnout? While you can't take away someone's stress, offering support can help lighten their emotional load.

Listen

Before jumping into "fixing" mode, offer to listen to your friend or family member's difficulties.

Having someone to talk to can make a world of difference. Often people need someone to witness their stress and suffering, and listening can go a long way.

Validate Feelings And Concerns

When friends and family members are feeling the effects of burnout, saying *it doesn't sound that bad* or *i'm sure things will get better* — while meant to offer reassurance — can feel invalidating if someone is feeling low and hopeless.

Instead, offer validation by saying, "you've been working so hard, i can understand why you feel depleted."

Offer Specific Types Of Help

Individuals who are burnt out are often too tired to think of ways that others can help them. Instead of asking, "how can i help?" Offer to drop off a meal, pick up dry cleaning, or do a load of laundry.

Kind Gestures

Sending flowers, a thoughtful text message, or a written card can remind friends and family members that they're not alone.

Because they're often working long hours, people with burnout can feel lonely and underappreciated. But small gestures of kindness can be nurturing.

Research Resources

If friends or family members need additional support, like childcare, a house cleaner, or a psychotherapist, offer to research and crowdsource for specific resources to help ease the stress.

Being exposed to continual stress can cause us to burnout. Feelings of exhaustion, anxiety, and isolating from friends and family members can be some of the signs. However, eating a balanced diet, regular exercise, and getting a good night's sleep may prevent this stressed state.

Worried about friends and family members who may be burnt out? Listening to their concerns, validating their emotions, and offering specific types of support can help lighten the load.

Burnout can be avoided by making self-care part of your daily routine. Even if you're working long hours, studying for exams, or taking care of young children, remember to sprinkle some joy into each day.

Try going for a walk, talking to a friend, or watching an enjoyable program on television. Small self-care gestures like these can stop stress from turning into something more serious, like burnout.

Chapter 22:
10 Habits of Meryl Streep

Meryl Streep is an American actress known for her incomparable abilities; she can adapt to complicated accents, sing, be a comedian, and play old male rabbi. Meryl roles have brought her from African bush and Greece beaches, Julia Child's legendary kitchen, and Disney wonderland. If you have watched Meryl ace her roles, this doesn't sound like a standard joke. Meryl is undoubtedly a Hollywood queen with 21 Academy Award nominations and three wins for Kramer vs. Kramer, Sophie's Choice, and The Iron Lady. Rising to such fame, staying modest and brilliant, and, ahem-an an estimation of $ 160 million net-worth, Meryl maintains specific principles.

Here are 10 habits of Meryl Streep to enumerate from.

1. Focus on the Skills Rather Than Looks

During an interview with Vogue, Meryl said that stressing about your weight or skin will derail you. Instead, concentrate on what you enjoy doing, as what you put your hands on should be your world. Meryl had repeatedly reiterated her stance on choosing genius over beauty, even when told she is "too ugly."

2. Focus on the Bigger Picture

It is natural for people to succumb to the muck of stress, deadlines, and anxiety. It is also common to find yourself overcommitting or doubting whether you can do a task or achieve a specific goal. However, if you take a step back and breathe, you will see the bigger picture. Meryl said that the one thing she could tell her 20-something old self would be to think big. She wished she could have devoted more time comprehending the critical role she had in society.

3. Be Authentic

Never, ever apologize for being true to yourself. Meryl was called fat, ugly, and her nose being ridiculed. She recalls how at first, her self-esteem declined to a point she couldn't even watch her shows but later made it her aim to criticize societal expectations of a slim, perfect, and beautiful goddess Hollywood queen.

4. Listen Always

Meryl studies accents as well as what they communicate to stay in tune with the roles she portrays. She achieves this by empathically listening. It means listening before and after work and in between work-to those you associate daily to learn, listening to everything.

5. Age Is Just a Number

Meryl insists on embracing your age and doing what you can utmost at any phase. She has always been vocal against Hollywood manifestations of stripping female actresses short. Meryl has used her influence to fight against ageism, demonstrating that women of all ages deserve to be heard, seen, and appreciated.

6. Start by Starting, Stay Consistent

In the 90s, Meryl kept on making moves despite getting zero Oscar nominations. You have to keep doing what you're doing. Just keep going no matter what.

7. Stay Connected With Your Family

If you are a mother and jogs between 8 to 10 working hours and attending to your family, you hold a soft spot in Meryl's heart. In a podcast, she recounts how her priority was only on those roles that were both location and time-friendly to have quality time with her family.

8. Make the Mold, Then Advance It

After developing an understanding of yourself, set your standards and navigate your way through, which you'll rely on. It is about what feels suitable to you, not what you've been told. Throughout her 45-year career, Meryl has created and reinvented herself, thus ensuring that she improves her talent, craft, and ideas and remaining relevant in Hollywood.

9. Good Things Take Time

In modern society, delayed progress is no progress, and the patient feels worthless than virtuous. Nonetheless, Meryl's career journey is an excellent example of how good things take time because it wasn't until 10 years after acting that she gained the recognition she deserved. Persist at it until you get to where you want to be.

10. Stay Humble

Meryl Streep often referred to as the best actress of her generation, would have within her rights succumbed to the luxuries of being a celebrity. But she chose to stay grounded, and as she told Vogue Magazine that she tried as much to live an ordinary life as when you do your own taming, you cannot get spoilt.

Conclusion

Having has built a successful career from the bottom through her appearances and roles in films and other avenues, Meryl Strip has become an iconic influence that seamlessly defines how you can hit the top by just being you.

Chapter 23:
Become A High Performer

We were put on this planet because we were meant to be all we could become. Human beings are the sum of their acts and achievements. But not everyone is capable of doing things to their full potential.

Every man's biggest burden is his or her unfulfilled potential.

So what you need to become a high-performing individual in this modern era of competition is to idolize the best of the best.

You will need to understand the real-life features of a successful individual and what you need to do to become one.

If you want to be more successful in your life you need to become obsessive. Start your day with a goal and try your best to achieve it before you head to bed. You don't necessarily need to be on the right path with the first step, but you will find the best route once you have the undefeated will to find that path.

If you want to be more developed in your life you need to sleep effectively. The most successful people have a mantra of high performing routine. They don't sleep more than five hours a day and work seven days a week. They only take one day a week to sleep more just to rejuvenate their brains and body.

If you want to know if you are a high-performing successful person, look into your body language. If you find ease and leisure in everyday tasks, You are surely not standing up to your potential. If you like to sit for a conversation, start to stand. If you like to walk, start running. Get out of your comfort zone and start thinking and acting differently.

The last thing before you start your search for the right path to excellence is to set a goal every day. Increase your creativity by finding new ways to shorten the time of you becoming the better you and finally getting what you deserve.

You will eventually start seeing your life get on the track of productive learning and execution.

Change your way of treating others, especially those who are below you. If you are not a jolly person when you are broke, you can never be a jolly person when you are rich.

Never underestimate someone who is below you. You never know to whom the inspiration might take you. You have to consider the fact that life is ever-changing. Nothing ever stays the same. People never stay where they are for long.

It is the alternating nature of life that makes you keep fighting and pushing harder for better days. That is why you work hard on your skills to become a hearty human with the arms of steel.

Most people live a quiet life of desperation where they have a lot to give and a lot to say but can never get out of their cocoons.

But you are not every other person. You are the most unique soul god has created to excel at something no one has ever thought or seen before.

Start loving yourself. Stop finding faults in yourself. You are the best version of yourself, you just haven't found the right picture to look into it yet.

You want to be a high performer in every aspect of your life, here is my final advice for you.

If you push your limits in even the smallest tasks of your life, if you stretch your mind and imagination, if you can push the rules to your benefit, you might be the happiest and the most successful man humankind has ever seen.

Keep working for your dreams till the day you die. Life opens its doors to the people who knock on it. The purpose of this life is to knock on every door of opportunity and grasp that opportunity before anyone else steps forward.

You won't fulfill your desires till you make the desired effort, and that comes with a strong will and character. So keep doing what you want to never have a regret.

Chapter 24:
The Downside of Work-Life Balance

One way to think about work-life balance is with a concept known as The Four Burners Theory. Here's how it was first explained to me:

Imagine that a stove represents your life with four burners on it. Each burner symbolizes one major quadrant of your life.

1. The first burner represents your family.
2. The second burner is your friends.
3. The third burner is your health.
4. The fourth burner is your work.

The Four Burners Theory says that "to be successful, you have to cut off one of your burners. And to be successful, you have to cut off two."

The View of the Four Burners

My initial reaction to The Four Burners Theory was to search for a way to bypass it. "Can I succeed and keep all four burners running?" I wondered.

Perhaps I could combine two burners. "What if I lumped family and friends into one category?"

Maybe I could combine health and work. "I hear sitting all day is unhealthy. What if I got a standing desk?" Now, I know what you are thinking. Believing that you will be healthy because you bought a standing desk is like believing you are a rebel because you ignored the fasten seatbelt sign on an airplane, but whatever.

Soon I realized I was inventing these workarounds because I didn't want to face the real issue: life is filled with tradeoffs. If you want to excel in your work and your marriage, then your friends and your health may have to suffer. If you want to be healthy and succeed as a parent, then you might be forced to dial back your career ambitions. Of course, you are free to divide your time equally among all four burners, but you have to accept that you will never reach your full potential in any given area.

Essentially, we are forced to choose. Would you rather live a life that is unbalanced but high-performing in a certain area? Or would you rather live a life that is balanced but never maximizes your potential in a given quadrant?

Option 1: Outsource Burners

We outsource small aspects of our lives all the time. We buy fast food, so we don't have to cook. We go to the dry cleaners to save time on laundry. We visit the car repair shop, so we don't have to fix our automobile.

Outsourcing small portions of your life allow you to save time and spend it elsewhere. Can you apply the same idea to one quadrant of your life and free up time to focus on the other three burners?

Work is the best example. For many people, work is the hottest burner on the stove. It is where they spend the most time, and it is the last burner to get turned off. In theory, entrepreneurs and business owners can outsource the work burner. They do it by hiring employees.

The Four Burners Theory reveals a truth everyone must deal with: nobody likes being told they can't have it all, but everyone has constraints on their time and energy. Every choice has a cost.

Which burners have you cut off?

Chapter 25:
<u>10 Habits to Change Your Life</u>

I'm sure everyone wonders at a certain point in their life that what is the thing that is stopping them from reaching their goals. It is your bad and unhealthy habits that hold you down. If you want to succeed in life, you need to get rid of these habits and adopt healthy habits to help you in the long run.

Here are 10 healthy habits that will change your life completely if you can adopt them in your daily life:

1. Start Following a Morning Ritual

Everyone has something that they love to do, i.e., things that boost their energy and uplifts their mood. Find one for yourself and do that every morning. It will help you kickstart your day with a bright and cheerful mood. It will also help you to eliminate mental fatigue and stress. You will find yourself super energetic and productive. Let me tell you some morning rituals that you can try and get benefitted from.

- *Eating Healthy:* If you are very passionate about health and fitness, eating healthy as a morning ritual might be a win-win situation for you. You can have a nutritious breakfast every morning. Balance your breakfast with proper amounts of carbs, fats, proteins, etc. It will not only help you in staying healthy but will also help you kickstart your day on a proactive note.

- *Meditating:* Meditation is an excellent way of clearing your mind, enhancing your awareness, and improving your focus. You can meditate for 20 to 30 minutes every morning. Then you can take a nice warm shower, followed by a fresh cup of coffee. Most importantly, meditating regularly will also help you strengthen your immune system, promote emotional stability, and reduce stress.

- *Motivating:* A daily dose of motivation can work wonders for you. When you are motivated, your productivity doubles, and you make the best out of your day. Every morning, you can simply ask yourself questions like, "If it is the last day of your life, what do you want to do?", "What productive thing can I do today to make the best out of the day" "What do I need to do in order to avoid regretting later for having wasted a day?". When you ask yourself questions like these, you are actually instructing your brain to be prepared for having a packed-up and productive day.

- *Writing:* Writing can be a super-effective way of kickstarting your day. When you journal all your thoughts and emotions every day after waking up, it allows you to relieve yourself from all the mental clutter, unlocks your creative side, and sharpens your focus.

- *Working Out:* Working out is a great morning ritual that you can follow every day. When you work out daily, it helps you burn more fat, improves your blood circulation, and boosts your energy level. If you are interested in fitness and health, this is the perfect morning ritual for you. You can do some cardio exercises, or some strength training, or both. Depending on your suitability, create a workout routine for yourself and make sure to stick to that. If you don't stick to your routine, it won't be of much help.

-

2. Start Following the 80/20 Rule

The 80/20 rule states that almost 20% of the tasks you perform are responsible for yielding 80% of the results. It is why you should invest more time in tasks that can give you more significant results instead of wasting your time on tasks that yield little to no results. In this way, you can not only save time but also maximize your productivity. Most importantly, when you see the results after performing those tasks, you will be more motivated to complete the following tasks. After you have finished performing these tasks, now you can quickly move your concentration and focus towards other activities that you need to do throughout your day.

3. Practice Lots of Reading

Reading is a great habit and a great way to stimulate your creativity and gaining more knowledge. When you get immersed in reading, it calms you and improves your focus, almost similar to meditating. If you practice reading before going to bed, you are going to have a fantastic sleep. You can read non-fiction books, which will help you seek motivation, develop new ideas, and broaden your horizon. You can also get a lot of advice about how to handle certain situations in life.

4. Start Single-tasking

Multitasking is hard, and almost 2% of the world's total population can do this properly. You can try multitasking occasionally. If you keep on trying to do this all the time, it will form a mental clutter, and as a result, your brain won't be able to filter out unnecessary information. Many studies have suggested that it can severely damage your cognitive control and lower your efficiency when you multitask a lot. It is the main reason why you should try to do single-tasking more than multitasking. Prepare a list of all the tasks you need to perform in a day and start with the most important one. Make sure not to rush and to complete one thing at a time.

5. Start Appreciating More

Appreciating things is totally dependent on your mentality. For example, some people can whine and complain about a glass being half empty, whereas some people appreciate that there is half a glass of water. It totally depends on your point of view and way of thinking. People get blinded by the urge to reach success so much that they actually forget to appreciate the little things in life. If you are working and earning a handsome salary, don't just sit and complain about why you are not earning more, what you need to do to achieve that, etc. You should obviously aim high, but not at the cost of your well-being. When you practice gratitude, it increases your creativity, improves your physical health, and reduces your stress. You can start writing about the things you are grateful for in your journal every day before going to bed, make some time for appreciating your loved ones, or remind yourself of all the things you are grateful for before going to bed every day. If you are not happy with your current situation, you will not be happy in the future. You need to be happy and satisfied at first, and then only you can work on progressing further.

6. Always Keep Positive People Around You

When you have toxic people around you, it gets tough for you to stay in a good mood or achieve something good in life. Toxic people always find a way to pull you down and make you feel bad about yourself. You should always surround yourself with people who are encouraging and positive. When you do that, your life is going to be full of positivity.

7. Exercise on a Regular Basis

Start exercising regularly to maintain good health and enhancing your creativity and cognitive skills. It also increases your endurance level and boosts your energy. When you exercise regularly, your body produces more endorphins. These hormones work as anti-depressants.

8. Start Listening More

Effective communication is very important in maintaining both professional and personal relationships. For communicating effectively, you need to work on your listening capability first. You need to pay attention to the things said by others instead of focusing only on what you have to say. Listening to others will allow you to understand them better. When you listen to someone, it makes them understand that they are valued and that you are here to listen to them. When they feel important and valued, they also start paying attention to what you say, thereby contributing to effective communication. Don't try to show fake concentration while you are busy thinking about something else. When you listen more, you learn more.

9. Take a Break from Social Media (Social Media Detox)

Many studies have shown that excessive use of social media can contribute to depression. Most importantly, it wastes a lot of time because people meaninglessly scroll, swipe, and click for hours. It is a very unhealthy habit and is very bad for bothe physical and mental health. Sometimes you need to completely stop using social media for a while to reduce mental clutter and stress. Turn off your laptops and phones every day for a few hours. It will help you to reconnect with the surrounding world and will uplift your mood.

10. Start Investing More in Self-care

Make some time for yourself out of your busy schedule. It is going to boost your self-esteem, improve your mental health, and uplift your mood. You need to do at least one thing for yourself every day that will make you feel pampered and happy. You can prepare a mouth-watering meal, take a comfortable bubble bath, learn something new, or just relax while listening to music.

The moment you start introducing these habits in your daily, you will instantly see change. Remember that even a tiny step towards a positive change can give outstanding results if you stay consistent.

Chapter 26:
8 Ways To Gain Self-Confidence

Confidence is not something that can be inherited or learned but is rather a state of mind. Confidence is an attribute that most people would kill to possess. It comes from the feelings of well-being, acceptance of your body and mind (your self-esteem), and belief in your ability, skills, and experience. Positive thinking, knowledge, training, and talking to other people are valuable ways to help improve or boost your confidence levels. Although the definition of self-confidence is different for everyone, the simplest one can be 'to have faith and believe in yourself.'

Here are 8 Ways To Gain More Self-Confidence:

1. Look at what you have already achieved:

It's easy to lose confidence when we dwell on our past mistakes and believe that we haven't actually achieved anything yet. It's common to degrade ourselves and not see our achievements as something special. But we should be proud of ourselves even if we do just a single task throughout the day that benefited us or the society in any way. Please make a list of all the things you are proud of, and it can be as small as cleaning your room or as big as getting a good grade or excelling in your job. Keep adding your small or significant achievements every day. Whenever you feel low in confidence, pull out the list and remind yourself how far you have come, how many amazing things you have done, and how far you still have to go.

2. Polish the things you're already good at:

We feel confident in the things we know we are good at. Everyone has some kind of strengths, talents, and skills. You just have to recognize what's yours and work towards it to polish it. Some people are naturally good at everything they do. But that doesn't make you any less unique. You have to try to build on those things that you are good at, and they will help you built confidence in your abilities.

3. Set goals for yourself daily:

Whether it's cooking for yourself, reading a book, studying for a test, planning to meet a friend, or doing anything job-related, make a to-do list for yourself daily. Plan the steps that you have to take to achieve them. They don't necessarily have to be big goals; you should always aim for small achievements. At the end of the day, tick off all the things you did. This will help you gain confidence in your ability to get things done and give you a sense of self-appreciation and self-worth.

4. Talk yourself up:

That tiny voice inside of our heads is the key player in the game of our lives. You'll always be running low on confidence if that voice constantly has negative commentary in your mind telling you that you're not good enough. You should sit somewhere calm and quiet and talk to yourself out of all the negative things. Treat yourself like you would treat a loved one when they tend to feel down. Convince yourself that you can achieve anything, and there's nothing that can stop you. Fill your mind with positive thoughts and act on them.

5. Get a hobby:

Find yourself something that really interests you. It can either be photography, baking, writing, reading, anything at all. When you have found yourself something you are passionate about, commit yourself to it and give it a go. Chances are, you will get motivated and build skills more quickly; this will help you gain self-confidence as you would gradually get better at it and feel accomplished. The praises you will get for it will also boost your confidence.

6. Face your fears:

The best way to gain confidence is to face your fears head-on. There's no time to apply for a promotion or ask someone out on a date until you feel confident enough. Practice facing your fears even if it means that you will embarrass yourself or mess up. Remind yourself that it's just an experiment. You might learn that making mistakes or being anxious isn't half as bad as you would have thought. It will help you gain confidence each time you move forward, and it will prevent you from taking any risks that will result in negative consequences.

7. Surround yourself with positive people:

Observe your friends and the people around you. Do they lift you and accept who you are or bring you down and point out your flaws? A man is known by the company he keeps. Your friends should always positively influence your thoughts and attitude and make you feel better about yourself.

8. **Learn To Strike A Balance:**

Self-confidence is not a static measure. Some days, we might feel more confident than others. We might often feel a lack of confidence due to criticism, failures, lack of knowledge, or low self-esteem. While another time we might feel over-confident. We might come off as arrogant and self-centred to other people, and it can eventually lead to our failure. We should keep a suitable amount of confidence within ourselves.

Conclusion:

Confidence is primarily the result of how we have been taught and brought up. We usually learn from others how to behave and what to think of ourselves. Confidence is also a result of our experiences and how we learn to react in different situations. Everyone struggles with confidence issues at one time or another, but these quick fixes should enough to boost your confidence. Start with the easier targets, and then work yourself up. I believe in you. Always!

Chapter 27:
7 Ways To Discover Your Strengths

It is a fact that everybody has at least one skill, one talent, and one gift that is unique to them only. Everyone has their own set of strengths and weaknesses. Helen Keller was blind but her talent of speaking moved the world. Stephen Hawking theorised the genesis by sitting paralyzed in a wheelchair. The barber who does your hair must have a gifted hand for setting YOUR hair at reasonable prices—otherwise you wouldn't be visiting them.

See, the thing is, everyone is a prodigy at one thing or another. It's only waiting to be discovered and harnessed. Keeping that fact in mind…

Here are 7 Ways You can Discover Your Potential Strengths and Change Your Life Forever:

1. Try Doing Things That You Have Never Done

Imagine what would have happened if Elvis Presley never tried singing, if Michael Jordan never tried playing basketball or if Mark Zuckerberg never tried coding. These individuals would have been completely different persons, serving different purposes in life. Even the whole world would've been different today if some specific people didn't try doing some specific things in their lives.

Unfortunately, many of us never get to know what we are truly good at only because we don't choose to do new things. We don't feel the need to try and explore things that we have never done before in our lives. As a result, our gifted talents remain undiscovered and many of us die with it. So while the time is high, do as many different things you can and see what suits you naturally. That is how you can discover your talent and afterwards, it's only a matter of time before you put it to good use and see your life change dramatically.

2. Don't Get Too Comfortable With Your Current State

It is often the case that we cling on to our current state of being and feel absolutely comfortable in doing so. In some cases, people may even embrace the job that they don't like doing only because 'it pays enough'. And honestly, I totally respect their point of view, it's up to people what makes them happy. But if you ask me how one can discover their hidden talents—how one might distinguish oneself—then I'm going to have to say that never get used to doing one particular thing. If one job or activity occupies you so much that you can't even think of something else, then you can never go out to venture about doing new stuff. The key is to get out, or should I say 'break out' from what you are doing right now and move on to the next thing. What is the next thing you might want to try doing before you die? Life is short, you don't want to go on your whole life, never having experienced something out of your comfort bubble.

3. What Is The Easiest Thing You Can Do?

Have you ever found yourself in a place where you did something for the first time and immediately you stood out from the others? If yes, then chances are, that thing might be one of your natural strengths.

If you've seen 'Forrest Gump', you should remember the scene where Forrest plays table-tennis for the first time in a hospital and he's just perfect at the game. "For some reason, ping-pong came very naturally to me, so I started playing it all the time. I played ping-pong even when I didn't have anyone to play ping-pong with.", says Forrest in the movie.

So bottomline, pay attention to it if something comes about being 'too easy' for you. Who knows, you might be the world's best at it.

4. Take Self-Assessment Tests

There are countless, free self-assessment tests that are available online in all different kinds of formats. Just google it and take as many tests you like. Some of these are just plain and general aptitude tests or IQ tests, personality tests etc. while there are others which are more particular and tell you what type of job is suited for you, what kind of skills you might have, what you might be good at, and those kinds of things. These tests are nothing but a number of carefully scripted questions which reveal a certain result based on how you answered each question. A typical quiz wouldn't take more than 30 minutes while there are some short and long quizzes which might take 15 minutes and 45 minutes respectively.

Though the results are not very accurate, it can do a pretty good job at giving you a comprehensive, shallow idea of who you are and what you can be good at.

5. Make Notes On How You Deal With Your Problems

Everyone faces difficult situations and overcomes them in one way or the other. That's just life. You have problems, you deal with them, you move on and repeat.

But trouble comes in all shapes and sizes and with that, you are forced to explore your problem-solving skills—you change your strategies and tactics—and while at it, sometimes you do things that are extraordinary for you, without even realizing it. John Pemberton was trying out a way to solve his headache problem using Coca leaves and Kola nuts, but incidentally he made the world's coke-drink without even knowing about it. Lesson to be learned, see how YOU deal with certain problems and why is it different from the others who are trying to solve the same problem as you.

6. Ask Your Closest Friends and Family

People who spend a lot of time with you, whether it be your friend, family or even a colleague gets to see you closely, how you work, how you behave, how you function overall. They know what kind of a person you are and at one point, they can see through you in a manner that you yourself never can. So, go ahead and talk to them, ask them what THEY think your strongest suit can be—listen to them, try doing what they think you might turn out to be really good at, Who knows?

7. Challenge Yourself

The growth of a human being directly corresponds to the amount of challenge a person faces from time to time. The more a person struggles, the more he or she grows—unlocks newer sets of skills and strengths. This is a lifelong process and there's no limit on how far you can go, how high your talents can accomplish.

Now, one might say, "what if I don't have to struggle too much? What if my life is going easy on me?". For them, I'd say "invite trouble". Because if you are eager to know about your skills and strengths (I assume you are since you're reading this), you must make yourself face difficulties and grow from those experiences. Each challenge you encounter and overcome redefines your total strength.

Final Thoughts

To sum it up, your life is in your hands, under your control. But life is short and you gotta move fast. Stop pursuing what you are not supposed to do and set out to find your natural talents RIGHT NOW. Once you get to know your strengths, you will have met your purpose in life.

Chapter 28:
7 Ways To Know When It's Time To Say Goodbye To The Past

Holding on to someone or something and fearing to let go is a problem that many of us will struggle with at some point or another. Be it a partner, career, or item, a history has been built around that and we find it hard to move on and leave this treasured piece behind.

Whether it be a 6months or 10 years, it can be hard for us to come to terms with letting go because we have invested so much time, energy, and soul, into it. Governed by emotions, we hold on to them even though it may no longer bring us happiness or joy.

Whatever the reasons are, here are 7 ways that can help you say goodbye to the past and invite better things into your life:

1. You've Drag things For Way Too Long

If it's a career that you're holding on to, you may feel that you've invested a lot of effort and energy in it, waiting for the time that you will get promoted. But the days come and go, months turn into years, and you find yourself a decade later wondering what happened. Letting things drag on is no way to live life. Time is precious and every moment we waste is a moment we can never get back.

2. You Know It's Time

People may tell us we're happy and that we should be so lucky to have this job or that person in our lives, but no one can hide the unhappiness that is festering within us. Deep down in our hearts, we understand ourselves more than any other people ever would. And we know, subconsciously, if it's time to move on and let go of the past. If you are unsure, do some soul-searching. Find a time to sit by yourself quietly, or go for a retreat on your own. Sort out your feelings and bring some clarity to yourself.

3. It No Longer Brings You Joy

With a person who we have spent so much energy being a relationship with over the years, it can be hard to come to terms with the reality that he or she no longer makes you feel happy or loved anymore. Being in a constant state of unhappiness is no way to live our lives. We have every power in us to make decisions that serves us rather than hinder us. Acknowledge and accept these feelings of unhappiness. Use it as fuel to make that important decision that you know you must make.

4. You Are Holding On Out of Fear

Many a times we hold out on ending that relationship with something because we live in a constant state of fear. Career-wise we may resign ourself to the fate that things are just the way it is and we are afraid that we may never find another job again. So we hold on to that false sense of security and just drag your feet till retirement. Relationship wise, we hold on to them because we fear we may never find someone else again. So we let fear keep us in these places, feeling more and more trapped in the process.

5. You're Afraid of the Unknown

It is human nature to be afraid of the unknown. If we cannot see a clear path ahead, most of us would not dare to travel down that road. We don't know if the grass will be greener on the other side if we quit our jobs, and we don't know what the dating world will be like after being out of it for so long. We lose confidence in believing the unknown is a magical place and that wonderful things can happen there if we let ourselves take the leap of faith. That was how we got to where we were in the first place before we realized it no longer served us anymore.

6. You're Ready For Change

This is similar to the second point about knowing it's time with one key difference - you know that you ready for a new phase of life. Having the urge to intact change in your life, you believe that you don't want to be stuck in whatever situation you are in anymore. You desperately want to make things better. Embrace these feelings and start taking strong action to force change to happen for you.

7. You Know You Deserve Happiness

Happiness has to be earned. Happiness doesn't just happen to you. If you know you deserve to be happy, and that the current thing you are holding on to only brings you sorrow, it is time to let it go. Only when you let go of what's holding you down can you make room for better and brighter things. Putting yourself out there in the face of trials and errors is the only way you can find what you are truly looking for. Demand happiness and expect it to happen to you.

Conclusion

Saying goodbye to the past is not easy, and not everyone has the courage or strength to do it. You can either choose to live in fear, or you can choose to live a brave life. It is time to make that critical decision for yourself at this crossroad right now. Only one choice can bring you the life that you truly desire. So choose wisely.

Chapter 29:
Dealing With Addictions

People engaging in addictive behavior go on to develop an actual addiction. They find that overcoming it is more challenging than they had expected. Most people believe that addiction is A myth and they can quit any time they want to, or they feel that they are an exception to the rule. It's only when they have completely fallen into the trap do they find themselves completely screwed. This is more likely with non-substance or behavioural addictions like - excessive eating, sex, gambling, shopping, and even exercise. What makes it more harmful and complicated is that for every addictive behaviour, some people can engage in the behaviour without developing an addiction.

Most people think that they are one of the lucky few who won't get hooked. But unfortunately, they don't realize the truth until it's too late. By the time they recognize the need for change, they may not even want to. It takes years of being faced with the negative consequences of an addiction before realizing that it might be causing significant problems.

Sooner or later, most people who have an addiction should decide that A change is necessary. Once they have made the decision and set up A specific goal in their mind, like quitting entirely or quitting only A portion of it from time to time, they can get A head start to work in that direction. Getting clear on your goal before putting it into practice is helpful for success in overcoming your addictions. Although quitting entirely may be the best path to wellness, reducing or eliminating the most harmful substances first is still A huge improvement and will greatly reduce the harm caused.

Once you get clear on your goal, you are still asked to prepare yourself for the change. Preparations might include removing addictive substances from your home and work, as well as eliminating any triggers in your life that may ensure you use those substances again. Suddenly quitting an addictive behaviour can be lonely, especially when you lose touch with people who don't indulge in the same behaviours. Take out time to contact friends and family who will support you in your goals without being judgemental. Find people who will take care of you when you slip up. Lose all those negative friends with whom you drink, use drugs, or engage in any addictive behaviours.

Quitting an addictive behaviour is never easy, and there is no right way to feel while you are quitting. You will feel like going back to your old habits, and you will find yourself depressed and cut off from the world. But that's okay. Give yourself time and re-evaluate yourself. If you start to feel like this, all is too overwhelming for you, and you can try different treatments that can help you to overcome your addiction. They can either be medical or psychological. There is no right type of treatment, and you have to decide for yourself which treatment is suiting you best. Cognitive behaviour therapy (cbt) helps many people. Research shows it is quite effective in helping people to deal with and overcome all kinds of addictions. You can also always consult A psychologist/psychiatrist to discuss your thoughts and seek medications.

Long-term recovery is an ongoing process of facing and coping with life without retreating into addictive behaviours. It's not the final destination. Seek help when you need it. Be proud of yourself and understand that you have come A long way and still have A long way to go.

Chapter 30:
Happy People Dream Big

Remember being a kid, and when somebody asked you what you wanted to be after growing up, you answered with a big dream: an astronaut, a ballerina, a scientist, a firefighter, or the President of the United States. You believed that you could achieve anything you set your mind at that no dream is too big that if you wanted, you would make it happen. But why is it that so many adults forget what it is like to dream big. Happy people are dreamers; if you want to become a happy person, you need to make dreaming big a habit; some people even say that if your dreams do not scare you, you are not dreaming big. Now you must be wondering how dreaming big can make you happy. Firstly, it helps you see that if you had a magic wand and you could get whatever you wanted, what you would want for yourself, and there is a chance that these dreams are things you want to achieve in your life somehow other. Secondly, it will help you in removing any fears you have about not being able to achieve your dreams because when you dream big, you think about what you want in your ideal world, and your fear will not come in your way because you would feel like you are living in that fantasy world. Lastly, you will put your dreams and desires into the universe, and the likelihood of making those dreams come true increases. Fulfilling your dreams makes you happy because you will be able to get what you have yearned for so long, and a sense of achievement will make you feel confident about yourself and the dream you had. Now you must have a question what should I do to start dreaming big I am going to outline some of the things you can practice!

Sit back, clear your mind and think about your desires and dreams. What do you want in life? If you had three wishes from a genie, what are the things you would ask for? What is something you would if no one was looking or if you weren't afraid. Now write these dreams down on a piece of paper. This way, they would seem more real. The next thing you should do is start reading some inspirational books that motivate you to start living your best life starting today! Lastly, make a list of goals you want to achieve and start working on them.

Chapter 31:
Be Motivated by Challenge

You have an easy life and a continuous stream of income, you are lucky! You have everything you and your children need, you are lucky! You have your whole future planned ahead of you and nothing seems to go in the other direction yet, you are lucky!

But how far do you think this can go? What surety can you give yourself that all will go well from the start to the very end?

Life will always have a hurdle, a hardship, a challenge, right there when you feel most satisfied. What will you do then?

Will you give up and look for an escape? Will you seek guidance? Or will you just give up and go down a dark place because you never thought something like this could happen to you?

Life is full of endless possibilities and an endless parade of challenges that make life no walk in the park.

You are different from any other human being in at least one attribute. But your life isn't much different than most people's. You may be less fortunate or you may be the luckiest, but you must not back down when life strikes you.

This world is a cruel place and a harsh terrain. But that doesn't mean you should give up whenever you get hit in the back. That doesn't mean you don't catch what the world throws at you.

Do you know what you should do? Look around and observe for examples. Examples of people who have had the same experiences as you had and what good or bad things did they do? You will find people on both extremes.

You will find people who didn't have the courage or guts to stand up to the challenge and people who didn't have the time to give up but to keep pushing harder and harder, just to get better at what they failed the last time.

The challenges of life can never cross your limits because the limits of a human being are practically infinite. But what feels like a heavy load, is just a shadow of your inner fear dictating you to give up.

But you can't give up, right? Because you already have what you need to overcome this challenge too. You just haven't looked into your backpack of skills yet!

If you are struggling at college, go out there and prove everyone in their wrong. Try to get better grades by putting in more hours little by little.

If people take you as a non-social person, try to talk to at least one new person each day.

If you aren't getting good at a sport, get tutorials and try to replicate the professionals step by step and put in all your effort and time if you truly care for the challenge at hand.

The motivation you need is in the challenge itself. You just need to realize the true gains you want from each stone in your path and you will find treasures under every stone.

Chapter 32:
10 Habits of Adele

There's no denying it, Adele Laurie Blue Adkins, better known as Adele is a musical legend. She is an English singer-songwriter and all-time great vocalist with excellent lyrical and passionate composing skills. Adele is one of the world's best-selling music artist, having sold over 120 million records worldwide.

With her exceptional voice and songwriting skills, the singer from a rough side of the town has captivated the hearts of millions of people. Adele got her admiration as an award-winning music legend, but moreover, there is much more from a lady who has overcome adversity to reach the top.

Here are 10 habits of Adele that will serve your learning journey.

1. It's Far From Easy

Criticism came thick and quick after Adele signed her first record deal because of her physical appearance. Many people, including Record label executives and high-profile designers publicly chastised her as "too fat" while suggesting weight loss to attract a larger fan base. Adele didn't let such criticism weigh in her talent as she unapologetically made hits after hits. Just like Adele, don't try to be anything or anyone but yourself.

2. Commitment Is Success

Despite constant pressure from the media to conform to their ludicrous notions of what women in the spotlight should look like, Adele chose her path and remained committed to being herself. This honesty is one of the attributes that Adele's fans admire. Such personality traits will breed your success.

3. It's Okay To Be Sad After a Breakup

When a relationship ends, you believe in acting tough and putting on a solid face. You're convinced on being tough to appear as you're suffering less than your ex-partners to win in some way. Adele defies expectations by telling her exes and the rest of the world about her grief without fear. She exemplifies humanity and vulnerability through her music.

4. Don't Take Life Too Seriously

It's okay to laugh at yourself or a hilarious scenario from time to time. Whether she's being teased in an interview or asked whether she wants to be a Bond Girl, Adele always respond with "Hahaha". She is quick to laugh, and her laugh is contagious.

5. Adversity Doesn't Stop Anything

Allow your pain to drive your mission. What if Adele waited till everything was back to normal before recording? All in all, people rushed to get her music, which she recorded in her misery. Every minute, every day, life happens and so should you commit to completing your projects without unconditionally.

6. Mirror Your Brand To Reflect Longevity

Say it quietly: Adele's tracks would have hit ten, twenty, or even fifty years ago. To call them timeless is a bit of a stretch. The fact may be that they're essentially personal because we believe that her music is basically from her life or personal experiences. However, Adele is always true to herself and then she sings authentically which is a formidable brand blend.

7. There Are Other Better Places Than the Spotlight

Adele doesn't constantly boost her social media presence and create "news" for constant consumption. Instead, she vanishes to do bizarre things like live and breathe and then reappears when she has something she hopes people would appreciate. It's tempting to feel the need to keep fulfilling it, but according to Adele, being true to yourself is more fulfilling.

8. Build Your Team, Not Just Yourself

When a technical issue nearly derailed her performance at Grammy Awards, Adele didn't cast an evil eye at her sound engineer. Not only did she make herself appear good by ending her performance properly, she also made her entire team look excellent. The question is, what do you do when life tosses you a curveball that you can't control?

9. Keep Going

Even when things are out of your control, it's easy to quit when everything seems to go wrong. But your perseverance will be rewarded!

10. Remember Where You Came From

Don't let your past or upbringing hold you back from achieving your goals in the future. Success is defined not by what you have as a child but by your level of commitment and work ethic over time. However, once you get there, don't forget where you come from.

Conclusion

You are characterized not by your physical appearance but by how you treat people and the words you use while communicating with everyone. Hence, just like Adele, have the confidence to pursue your aspirations. You never know where the road may take you.

Chapter 33:
Why Are You Working So Hard

Your why,

your reason to get up in the morning,

the reason you act,

really is everything - for without it, there could be nothing.

Your why is the partner of your what,

that is what you want to achieve, your ultimate goal.

Your why will be what pushes you through the hard times on the path to your dreams.

It may be your children or a burning desire to help those less fortunate,

whatever the reason may be,

it is important to keep that in mind when faced with troubles or distractions.

Knowing what you want to do, and why you are doing it,

is of imperative importance for your life.

The tragedy is that most people are aiming for nothing.

They couldn't tell you why they are working in a certain field even if they tried.

Apart from the obvious financial payment,

They have no clue why they are there.

Is financial survival alone really a good motive to act?
Or would financial prosperity be guaranteed if you pursued greater personal preference?
Whatever your ambitions or preference in life,
make sure your why is important enough to you to guarantee your persistence.

Sometimes when pursuing a burning desire,
we can become distracted from the reason we are working.

Your why should be reflected in everything you do.
Once you convince yourself that your reason is important enough, you will not stop.
Despite the hardships, despite the fear, despite the loss and pain.
As long as you maintain a steady path of faith and resilience,
your work will soon start to pay off.
A light will protrude from the darkness and the illusionary troubles sent to test your faith will disappear as if they were never here.

Your why must be strong.
Your what must be as clear as the day is to you now.
And your faith must be eternal and unwavering.
Only then will the doors be opened to you.
This dream can be real, and will be.

When it is clear in the mind with faith, the world will move to show you the way.
The way will be revealed piece by piece, requiring you to take action and do the required work to bring your dream into reality.

Your why is so incredibly important.
The bigger your why, the greater the urgency, and the quicker your action will be.

Take the leap of faith.
Do what you didn't even know you could.
Never mind anyone else.
Taking the unknown path.
Perhaps against the advice of your family and friend,
But you know what your heart wants.

You know that even though the path will be dangerous, the reward will be tremendous.
The risks of not never finding out is too great.
The risk of never knowing if you could have done better is unfathomable.
You can always do better, and you must.

Knowing what is best for you may prove to be the most important thing for you.
How you feel about the work you are doing,
How you feel about the life you are living,
And how do you make the most of the time you have on this earth.

These may prove far more important than financial reward could ever do for you.

Aim to strike a balance.
A balance between working on what you are passionate about and building a wealthy financial life.
If your why and will are strong enough,
Success is all but guaranteed for you – no second guesses needed.

Aim for the sky,
However high you make it,
you will have proven you can indeed fly.

Chapter 34:
Happy People Live Slow

"Slow Living means **structuring your life around meaning and fulfilment**. Similar to 'voluntary simplicity and 'downshifting,' it emphasizes a **less-is-more approach**, focusing on the quality of your life...Slow Living addresses the desire to lead a more balanced life and pursue a **more holistic sense of well-being** in the fullest sense of the word. In addition to the personal advantages, there are potential **environmental benefits** as well. When we slow down, we often use fewer resources and produce less waste, both of which have a lighter impact on the earth."

Slow living is a state of mind it will make you feel purposeful and is more fulfilling. It is all about being consistent and steady. Now that you have an idea of slow living, we will break down some myths attached to slow living and how to start slow living for mind peace and happiness. The first myth is that slow living is about doing everything as slowly as possible. Slow living is not about doing everything in slow motion but doing things at the right speed and not rushing. It is all about gaining time so you can do things that are important to you. The second myth is that slow living is the same as simple living. Now simple living is more worldly, and simple living is more focused on time.

The third myth is that slow living is an aesthetic that you see on desaturated Instagram posts, but that is not true; this is considered a minimalist aesthetic, whereas slow living is a minimalist lifestyle. The 4th myth is that slow living is about doing and being less. That is not at all true. It is all about removing the non-essentials from your life so you can have more time to be yourself. And the last myth is that slow living is anti-technology now. This is not about travelling back in time but all about using tech as a tool and not vice versa.

If you like this idea of living, we are going to list ten ways in which you can start slow living;

1. Define what is most important to you(essentials)
2. Say no to everything else (non-essentials)
3. Understand busyness and that it is a choice
4. Create space and margin in your day and life
5. Practice being present
6. Commit to putting your life before work
7. Adopt a slow information diet
8. Get outside physically and connect dots mentally
9. Start slow and small by downshifting
10. Find inspiration in the slow living community

Sit back and think about what the purpose of your life is, what you ultimately want from your life and not just in a monetary sense. Think about what you would like for your lifestyle to be 50 years from now, and then start working on it today. Suppose you have not figured out the purpose. In that case, there are multiple personality tests available on the internet that will help you determine your personality type and then eventually help you create your purpose.

Chapter 35:
Six Ways To Track Your Habits

We are mostly at the front line to judge other people based on their habits and behavior but when it comes to ourselves, there is where we draw the line. We become blind to our habits unless someone else points them out for us. Even if they do, we see their assessment of us as unfair and biased. This is not surprising because such is typical human behavior.

However, how can we assess ad track our habits instead of other people doing it for us? Here are six ways to track your habits:

1. Have A Mentor

A mentor is someone you look up to for leadership, guidance, and inspiration in your life. They are icons of character and success from whom you cmulate the positive aspects of their lives. Their importance and the major role they play in shaping our habits is impossible to overlook. You may have mentors for many reasons among them being character development. They contribute immensely in influencing us to develop new habits and as well as track them.

You can track your progress in the adoption of a new habit by gauging yourself with the one who influenced you into it. You can tell whether you are up to standard or out of order regarding your habits. Your mentor becomes the unit of measurement of your progress and you can adjust to fit in.

2. Develop A Routine

A routine is a predictable way of doing things. It is important to have a routine from which you will tell when you stray. Being predictable is not a bad idea entirely. It is a way of checking the boxes of what you have or have not done daily. A routine is important whenever you want to track your habits because it is not biased.

Developing a routine could be difficult but the merits outweigh its demerits. Through a routine, you can perfect desirable habits that you seek to adopt. Practice makes perfect so does the repetition of a habit routinely ingrain it in your personality.

3. Listen To Other People's Opinions About You

What do the people around you say? Have they or have they not observed any notable change in your habits? You would be throwing the baby with the bathwater if you disregard their voices about you. When you hear their opinion, you will know whether you are on or off track regarding the habits you are adopting.

Indeed, people's opinions are not always correct. It could be their perception and not the truth. Regardless, there lies sincerity in unbiased observations by other people on you. They are in a better position to note any change in your habits or routine. You can track your habits through their observations.

4. <u>Benchmark With Your Peers</u>

Your peers are the people with whom you began the journey of adoption of new habits together. Find out whether they are making progress or you are the one lagging. Anything that did not affect their progress and did to yours should concern you. If you have derailed, seek to address what is holding you back.

Through this way, you can hold yourself accountable for your setbacks and forge a way forward. Tracking your habits using your peers' progress challenges your judgment on issues and commitment to resolutions you have made. Do not shy from making a follow-up of your habits through them.

5. <u>Use The Calender</u>

It looks like an analog method of tracking your habits but it has been tried, tested, and proven. Mark important days on your calendar because it creates memories of your journey in changing your habits. It serves as a reminder of a decision you had made which you should pursue to the end.

The most suggested type of calendar is the tangible one because you can see it often unlike the ones in digital form. A calendar will be the silent judge to help you keep track of your habits. Its inaudible judgment will haunt you whenever you see it.

6. <u>Set Milestones</u>

A milestone will consist of a bunch of habits that you seek to adopt. When your eyes are set on a milestone, nothing will distract you away from it. Your focus and energy shall be on completing a milestone.

You can gauge your progress by how many milestones you successfully set and conquered. This will keep you on track when monitoring your habits.

It is advisable to follow these six ways to track your habits if you want to gauge your progress.

www.ingramcontent.com/pod-product-compliance
Lightning Source LLC
LaVergne TN
LVHW012025060526
838201LV00061B/4469